Crash Test Parents

the
LIFE-CHANGING
MADNESS

of TIDYING UP
AFTER CHILDREN

Other books in the Crash Test Parents series:

Parenthood: Has Anyone Seen My Sanity?
*Crash Test Parents Guide to Surviving a Year**
*Crash Test Parents Guide to Self-Esteem**

*Available only at www.racheltoalson.com/freebook

To see all the books Rachel has written, please click or visit the link below:
www.racheltoalson.com/store

Rachel Toalson

the LIFE-CHANGING MADNESS

of TIDYING UP AFTER CHILDREN

BATLEE PRESS

Batlee Press
PO Box 591596
San Antonio, TX 78259

Copyright ©2017 by Rachel Toalson
All rights reserved.

No part of this book may be reproduced or transmitted in any form or by any means, electronic or mechanical, including photocopying and recording, or by any information storage and retrieval system, without permission in writing. For information, address Batlee Press, PO Box 591596, San Antonio, TX 78259.

The author appreciates your taking the time to read her work. Please consider leaving a review wherever you bought it, or telling your friends how much you enjoyed it. Both of those help spread the word, which is incredibly important for authors. Thank you for your support.
www.racheltoalson.com
www.crashtestparents.com

Manufactured in the United States of America

First Edition—2017/Cover designed by Toalson Marketing
www.toalsonmarketing.com

To my children, who provided enough material to write this book
R.T.

Contents

Why Can't I Keep My House in Order? (Oh, Yeah. Kids.)
5

Always Discard First (Not Your Children. Your Stuff)
41

The Best Way to Tidy is By Category (Or How to Drive Yourself Insane)
79

Find a Place For Everything (It Won't Stay There, Of Course)
127

The Tidying Effort Transforms Your Life (Tidying Myths Debunked)
165

The Real Story of Tidying Up (Or What Kids Do to a Home)
197

Foreword

It was with an open mind and an open heart that I read Marie Kondo's *The Life-Changing Magic of Tidying Up*. And I think it's a valuable, important book for many people. It can help them achieve greater clarity in their lives and minimize the distractions they keep on hand in their homes by reducing what they own. But while I was reading it, I found myself laughing about how kids make nearly everything impossible when it comes to a tidy home—especially when we're talking about multiple kids. And I wondered why no one had written a humor book celebrating the maddening tendencies of messy children.

So when a book does not exist already, of course a writer is going to write it.

This book is not a prescriptive book. This book is simply a real-life look at a family that tried to live out the life-changing magic of tidying up. This book is a look at the humorous challenges a family has when it comes to keeping a tidy home.

Kids aren't really tidy beings. And busy parents don't really have the time to remind them every other second (because that's what it takes most of the time) to pick up their things and put them where they belong. No, your dirty socks don't belong on the stretch of floor three inches from the hamper (just a little more effort). No, your shoes don't belong on the table. No, your toys don't belong in my bath tub. On and on and on it goes. A house with children will live in a perpetual state of needing to be tidied.

Which was, quite honestly, a bit disappointing after having read Kondo's book. It promised me that I would never have to tidy again. And maybe it is possible to never tidy again if you're single and living alone, if you're someone who doesn't work from home, someone who doesn't plan on having kids. But for the people who have kids, it's an impossible feat. My kids go to school and bring a billion papers home every day. My kids behave well at school, so they get to pick a crappy toy from the teacher's treasure box, and where are we going to put it? My kids find nature and bring it all inside.

I didn't want to be a frustrated parent all the time, with my high expectation, we'll-never-have-to-tidy-ever-again goals.

So I decided to write a book that celebrates the humor and madness of trying to tidy up after children. It's my way of coping with the fact that I will probably never have a completely tidy house—not even after the kids leave the nest, because, let's be honest, I'll be way too tired. There's nothing so exhausting as raising a human being to be a decent person, and by the time I'm done with it, I probably won't even care about having a tidy house. It's overrated anyway.

I wasn't a very fun person when I was trying to control the mess. I walked around annoyed all the time that I had to put those books back on the home library shelf for the two-thousandth time today, and it wasn't even 8 a.m. I angrily put toothbrushes back in their little blue cup, every single day, when one 3-year-old twin decided he was going to smuggle them into his bed while my back was turned. I punctured my heels on LEGOs and cursed to myself.

And I wasn't a very nice person when I whined about my wasted effort and the messy tables and how hard it was just to keep the house remotely clean—as if tidying was more important than my relationship with my children—until one day, when I was scraping the gigantic spit balls off the walls of my guest bathroom, I realized the truth: Tidying isn't the end all and be all.

If all I'm doing is nagging my kids constantly, they're not going to want to be anywhere near me. I'm not going to want to be anywhere near me, either. We're going to sacrifice time and relationship and fun, and I want to have fun. I want to play. I want my home to look like children live here. Mostly.

Our Pinterest World and its "10 Tips for Tidying" and "8 Steps for Having a Cleaner Home" don't often tell us the freedom story that I want to share within these pages: That it's okay not to have a perfectly put together, perfectly tidy home. It's okay. Because kids live here, and they will not always live here, and one day (I know it's hard to imagine) we will miss the dirt they tracked in and the crayon art they left on their bedroom closet walls and the toothbrush hunt we have to do every night. One day we will revel in these memories.

My hope is that in these pages, you will find yourself. I hope you will learn and accept that you can excuse your family from the life-changing magic of tidying up, as good as it sounds. I hope you will find freedom from trying to be perfect parents who are always perfectly put together.

This book does not, however, mean that I've given up on a tidy house. I'll hold to my dream until that last boy leaves my home. But it's definitely not the most important thing anymore. It's not even in the top ten.

And that has been magnificently refreshing. I hope it is for you, too.

Why Can't I Keep My House in Order? (Oh, Yeah. Kids.)

You Can't Tidy If You've Never Learned How

"Just put your stuff away," my mom used to say. "Just put it away." And then louder. "PLEASE JUST PUT IT AWAY."

Just get it off the table, just get it out of my sight, just get it where it needs to go, because where it needs to go is not HERE, on the table where we will eat our meals. For God's sake, let me have this one little place. Please. This one little place.

That's what my mother was saying between the lines. (I know this now, because I'm a parent.)

Most days we heard these words as soon as we stepped through the door, because she knew our tendencies. I couldn't believe it, though. Here I was, walking in on shaky legs and lifting arms that felt more like pudding than muscle, because I'd just finished a grueling two-hour volleyball practice where I served and dove and hustled, and I couldn't possibly lift that fifteen-pound backpack (I took Advanced Placement classes that required 500-page textbooks instead of the traditional 300-pagers) any farther than the table. Didn't she understand how tired I was? And what was the big deal? A backpack on the table? I needed to do my homework anyway. Might as well leave it out, because I would need it in half an hour. I was never one for wasting energy—like walking my backpack the thirteen steps to my bedroom and bringing only the school books I needed back out.

The problem was, it wasn't just my backpack. It was also my

clarinet, which I most definitely did not practice at the kitchen table, and also the sweatshirt I'd pulled on while standing outside in the semi-cold wind (probably 70-degree wind or something ridiculous like that), waiting for the bus ride home and then taken off right after walking into the warmer house.

My mom tried so hard to keep a tidy house growing up. And as a kid, it was my job—not intentionally, of course—to undo all her work.

On weekends, she'd toss out those vague words: "Clean your room." What did that even mean? I didn't have a clue. It looked clean (enough) to me. Sure, there were the jeans I'd taken off a few minutes ago, trading them for my much more comfy athletic shorts with the elastic waistband, but the jeans were still clean, and I'd need to put them back on for the date I had later that night. Why make the effort? I was nothing if not efficient. And there were the CDs stacked in the corners, but at least they were stacked neatly, and there were the books strewn on the table beside my bed, but I knew exactly which one I was going to pull out next, and disturbing their "organization" would mean destroying my plan. There was the makeup still left out on my dresser. But it was all stuff I would need later, too, and she could surely see that, couldn't she?

When I went to college, I wasted no time leaving tiny dorm rooms for a larger apartment. I was broke, though, so I had to share a two-bedroom space with three other girls. It was my space, and suddenly I found that I cared.

I used to complain to my mom about how my roommates left their books on the table and plates in the sink and clothes on their beds or the back of the couch or the patio outside, how I'd had to eat my breakfast of a can of green beans (Hey, this is a book about tidying, not eating disorders. That's a subject for another book.) staring at a blue Jansport cross-body satchel.

She would listen patiently and murmur her generous, "I'm sorry you're having to deal with that, sweetie," and it took me a long, long time to see the irony in it. I'm sure she was secretly thinking that I was getting my due, because mothers get this weird (but normal) satisfaction from seeing their kids learn lessons they tried to teach the hard way (I'm waiting eagerly for it. That strong-willed boy? He's going to have some hellion kids, and I'll watch and support and murmur my own, "I'm so sorry you're having to deal with that, sweetie," and secretly I'll be thinking, "You want to read my journal about you? Because you were no cake walk either.").

She'd probably complained to my grandmother about the same things, and Memaw probably listened and murmured, "I'm so sorry, sweetie," too. Parenting always comes full circle.

One night, when I had finished complaining about how I was the only one out of all my roommates who ever did the dishes and picked up clothes to put on roommates' beds or apparently cared about the way my apartment looked at all, my mother said, "Maybe it's just preparation for a messy husband."

No way, I thought. No way was I going to marry a man who was THAT messy.

Famous last words.

What It's Like Living in the Middle of Mess

It's not that Husband is messy so much. It's just that he's a little absent-minded. He's the typical creative stereotype. He probably made the stereotype—that's how good he is at adhering to it. He gets something out and legitimately forgets to put it back away, because there are more important things on his mind.

We married on a hot and humid day in October. The next day, on our way to the airport to catch the plane out to Orlando, where we would honeymoon at Disney World, he misplaced his wallet because he forgot he'd left it in the pocket of last night's pants.

We began our marriage in a tiny 800-square-foot apartment that had two bedrooms, two bathrooms, and a living/dining area with a tiny little kitchen. We'd gotten so many wedding gifts, appliances and utensils and plate sets and towels and miscellany, that we quickly filled the second bedroom with "Stuff We Plan to Use When We Have a House." Because why throw it away? We might need it some day.

I spent the end of my days picking up clothes from the floor, putting shoes back where they went, returning the toothpaste to the medicine cabinet (because I hate clutter on counters). I told him I hated this habit and that I really wished he'd try picking up after himself, and he made a valiant effort for a time. Things got manageable almost.

And then we had kids. Six of them.

I've given up a little more every year.

I still dream of a tidy house. Especially those nights when I'm sprinting back up the stairs because I just turned off all the lights and there's a monster chasing me through the dark and I step squarely on a jack they left out from the game they played earlier today because it blended in with the carpet. Those are the moments I would like a tidy house the most.

But kids.

That's all that needs to be said.

But. Kids.

Kids and all they come with—the diapers, the clothes that fit and then don't three months later, the buckets of toys grandparents give them at every turn (especially the McDonalds ones. Can you please stop taking my kids to McDonalds? Not only is the food disgusting, but the toys are ridiculously annoying)—make it so hard to keep a tidy house that eventually we find ourselves settling for a can-almost-see-the-floor house.

I keep trying. I really do. I teach our boys the importance of Putting Things Away. I tell them we're only going to Play With One Thing At a Time. I show them what it means to Tidy Up. And when it still doesn't work, I get all mean mama and fling my take-it-all-away and "we're-going-to-donate-it" threats, and my boys look at me like I've just told them someone died.

Tidying isn't really worth the fight. I have more skin in the game than they do. I could get rid of all their toys tomorrow, and they would still manage to find some branches out back to play with. They'd also bring them inside and make a mess with them.

I won't say it's *impossible* to have a tidy home when you have children. But it's definitely not worth the effort I'd have to put in to try to solve all the problems in our house and keep things out that didn't belong in.

Once I was tidying our living room, and I found a jar of dead snails.

"What should I do with this?" I asked Husband.

He just shook his head.

I said a few words over them, dumped them out in the trash, and put the jar in the sink, to be washed out and used again another day, for God knows what.

Becoming a Parent is the Moment You Start to Reset Your Life

Kids come with a whole lot of stuff. Babies, too. There's the diaper bag and all the baby food and the clothes they throw up on fifteen times a day and the diaper blowouts that go all the way up the back. There are the burp clothes for the ones who are exceptional at spitting up—I have four of them—and there are the tiny little socks that always seem to get lost, like they are constantly playing hide and seek in the black holes of our house (we have thousands of them, apparently). There are the toys.

Oh, the toys.

After one kid, I held to my expectations fiercely. Everything will be put back where it goes. Nothing will be left on the floor. We most definitely will not have one of those houses that looked like we'd all been taken hostage by an outrageous collection of toys.

And then we had the first birthday.

When your kid is the first grandchild on both sides of the family, you're really in for it. This was over before it started.

Every month for half the year we celebrate a birthday in our house, and there are family and friends bringing gifts for which we have no more room. We've tried encouraging them to do other things—give experiences, where the kids get to go to a restaurant with their own gift card; give art supplies, which are always in high demand; or give lessons, like art or music or karate. We'll gladly take all that.

Toys, though, are just a nuisance in a house of six kids.

We recently did a major overhaul of our toys, because they had completely taken over the garage. We don't allow toys in bedrooms, because kids will play all night and their getting enough sleep is important to me, and, besides, they're little devils when they haven't slept long enough.

We had four million superheroes in a bin they never asked to play with, so we packed them all in a garbage sack to donate to another lucky little boy (or a thousand). We had fifteen billion cars that I narrowed down to eighty-eight. We had thousands of books, and even those I sorted through and donated the ones we no longer loved to the local bookstore.

And yet, still, my boys find a way to make a mess.

I used to think that we could do things together, like creating art or enjoying music or building a tower out of contraption planks, and, because of all the time I spent with them playing and engaging, my boys would happily clean it up and put it back where it belonged. But, as I've already said elsewhere in this book (but which will probably be repeated like a mantra throughout), kids have an inherent aversion to cleaning up. And hanging up clothes. And flushing toilets.

It's only a matter of time before you just give up.

It took boys four and five (twins!) to completely drown me and rip that dream of a clean and tidy house from my still-desperately-clutching fingers. We moved into a season of survival, just get them fed, just get them to bed, just get out of bed in the morning, if you can manage that, and the tidying was moved to the "unimportant things that no longer matter" list.

It's happened in a progression, though.

Kid 1: I can do this. Of course I can keep a tidy house. This is so easy. I only have to go behind him and pick up all hours of the day. Eventually he'll learn. We'll play cleanup games, with that cute little cleanup song, and he'll be glad to do it every time.

Kid 2: Okay. This is a little harder, but I still got this. It's just that as soon as I clean up this mess one made, and the other one dumps out another. There aren't enough hands to put it all back, but I have a solution. Sit them down to lunch, or put them down for naps, and we'll get it cleaned up in no time. Still easy. Mostly.

Kid 3: It's like a three-ring circus everywhere I look. One is throwing planks in the air so they bounce behind the couch and under the bookshelves, another just dumped out a puzzle with one thousand pieces that's way too hard for a 2-year-old, and the baby is pulling out the blocks I put away, because he wasn't done playing with them. Well, there's still nap time. Except I'm so exhausted that the last thing I feel like doing is cleaning up. Oh, well. I'll leave it for their dad. I feel like I've been run over by a train.

Kid 4 (and 5, for us): I give up. On EVERYTHING.

Kid 6: This is us. Don't mind the scooter you have to step over to get to our door. Don't mind the LEGOs all over the floor (just keep your shoes on and you won't even notice them). Don't look too closely at the kitchen floor. You know what? Go ahead and look. I don't even care.

Every now and then the dream comes back around, when I see a beautiful picture on Pinterest or I read some ridiculous article like "Never tidy again!" I start thinking that surely they're ready for the tidy-house training now. Now that they're older they'll care about walking around on a floor that doesn't reach out and trip them. It won't take that much work, because they've matured since the last time we tried.

Ha. Where we only barely survive in a messy house, children thrive in it. The messier the better. We send the kids away for a weekend and straighten all the books on their shelves and re-fold all the clothes in their drawers, and two seconds after they get back home it's just the way they left it, and we could kick ourselves for even wasting the energy on trying. Energy is precious when you're a parent. Why spend it tidying up all the time?

Tidying enthusiasts say that tidying helps you reset your life. I get that. It does.

It helps you reset it with lower expectations.

Now it's not about "perfectly tidy" but "good enough tidy." It looks like this:

1. You can walk on the floor. There's enough space between toys and discarded clothes and all.those.papers to put your feet, like a kid-made obstacle course. Fun, isn't it?

2. When company comes over, make the master bedroom a repository for the extra crap. You'll "clean it up later." Watch later never come and marvel at how quickly your room becomes a trash dump. Don't worry. In six months you can just throw it all away, because, guess what, no one's missed it in all that time. Natural selection.

3. The dust is only an inch thick, not two. Two inches would be totally gross.

4. Kids flushed the toilet at least once today.

5. The clothes on the bed don't impede sleep. They're like extra blankets.

This is good enough for me.

The Trick to a Tidy House is Putting Everything Away

One of the secrets to tidying is to make sure, every day, that everything finds its way back to its place (the first rule of tidying is that "everything has a place").

Kids are notoriously bad at putting things back where they belong. That means guess who has the privilege of doing this every single day for the rest of your life, or at least until your kid turns 18?

That's right. You.

It's delightful.

I know, because just this morning my 3-year-olds got out all the crayons in the art cabinet, and, even though they're supposed to stay in the little crystal cups all nice and tidy, they threw them all over the dining room while I was preoccupied with feeding their littlest brother (okay, I was reading), and then they made their coloring books fly a little, because they were bored with watching the boring sight of crayons crashing against the wall and breaking upon contact. Minutes later, when they got bored with this, they ambled over to the little book basket I put downstairs because they're not allowed upstairs in our library alone and I wanted them to still have access to books, since I'm a mom who believes in the value of reading, and they took out all the books and spread them on the floor like a book carpet and then proceeded to walk across them (which is absolutely not allowed in our home, either), and then, after all that (that's right.

I'm still not finished. Tired yet? I am. So tired.), they decided that the neatly folded pile of their brother's clothes draped along the back of the couch would look much better all over the floor.

We have a rule in our home that whoever makes the mess has to clean it up. I don't make many messes in my house, but I'm usually the one cleaning it up.

Mostly because when it comes time for the boys to clean up their mess, they're "just too tired." It's "way too much." It's "too overwhelming."

There's another rule in our home that if they make a mess of something and don't clean it up, like, say, crayons, they will not get to play with that toy or supply for three days.

They don't care about this rule, either.

We keep all the art supplies where our kids can reach them and play with them all the time, because we believe in a creative home with free play and constant access to what kids need to create and explore and build. That means they have at their ready access crayons, markers, scissors (dull-tip ones), pencils, and paper.

This is probably the majority of the problem. Do you know how much mess a kid can make in half an hour of art time? The 8-year-old will usually cut out puppets of the intricate kind and leave all the scrap pieces everywhere, if he's not sneaking into my material closet and swiping the bright green fabric he likes to pretend he can sew into a pillow. The 6-year-old usually has a whole stack of papers out and is trying to see how many math facts he can fit onto a page. The 3-year-olds are typically racing to see on how many pages they can put one tiny, almost unnoticeable pink scribble before someone will notice they're using up all the available paper. (Answer: about thirteen seconds.)

And when it comes to cleaning up these masterpieces, there really is too much.

My boys are actually, generally, pretty good about cleaning things up. Except when they're not. The times they're not, they'll forget to check under the couch for that Lightning McQueen car I saw them scoot under there, and it will be left out to be found at a later date, probably when the cars are taken away and suddenly we have three cars in the living room and no bin to be found.

Something is always left out. There will be a shape block stuck under the couch cushion, where no one thought to look, because who tries to make geometric snowflakes on the couch? There will be pattern play pieces stuck behind the bookshelves that you'll only realize are there when you're trying to put together a pattern with your 5-year-old for snuggle time and he's devastated that one of the blocks is missing. There will be clothes stuffed under a trundle bed, because 3-year-olds want to hide the fact that they got into their closet again. There will be books pulled down all over the floor, because the 8-year-old wanted to see how many books were in this series before he decides whether or not to read them. There will be shoes stuffed behind loveseats, because instead of taking them off like a normal human being, the 6-year-old decided he wanted to see if he could kick his foot hard enough to get his tennis shoe off. And he did.

These are the reasons we should just tell it like it is: Parents will tidy endlessly.

Even if we're teaching our boys to clean, they're not going to do it to a standard that will mean they never, ever have to tidy again.

They will never be able to reach that standard of perfection, because they're just kids.

Some days, keeping the art supplies where the boys can find them all is great. Sometimes it goes very, very badly. Sometimes, when we're too tired to supervise or we're just checking out because being a parent is really, really hard, that art table can look more like a water color explosion than a nice place to eat. And then, to top it off, right underneath that beautiful display is their daddy's shoes he left where he took them off.

Those are the days when I tell myself the truth: This job will never end.

You know what? At least everything has a place. At least there's that. Not that it will ever see that place. But The Place exists.

Two of the Most Surprising Secrets of Tidying

There are all kinds of secrets to tidying up when you're a parent. Secrets like "just don't have any toys" or "make your kids play outside all day" (which is what we did all day when we were kids, wasn't it?), or maybe less drastic secrets, like "keep the toys to a minimum so kids can do things like art and writing," although then you have to contend with all that paper. So maybe just let them sit in front of the television all day until they become we-can't-even-move zombies.

You know, whatever.

But there are two secrets of tidying that I did not expect even a little bit.

The first surprising secret: What you throw away will mysteriously reappear.

Oh, you threw away that nifty little flashlight some family member thought would be a hit, and of course it was, but it has the most annoying voice in the history of whining and it makes that pattern on the ceiling that will keep your kids awake all hours of the night because they imagine the pattern moving and winking at them? Well, it will come back five days later, and you'll wonder how in the world it walked from the trash bin to your pillow, where it is staring at you, challenging you to dare say a word about where it's been and how it got there.

Creepy, creepy toys.

Of course you'll try to throw it away again. You'll even tie the bag with a zip tie and take it yourself out to the trash receptacle. You'll watch the toy sink into a pile of banana peels and holey socks, and you'll grin a little to yourself, because you've won this time.

But it will be back. Because your kids will be out on their scooters, minding their own business, and one of them will accidentally graze the trash bin, and it's enough for that persistent toy to cry out, and they will recognize that noise, and they will go digging for it. In the trash. Where you just tossed a diaper with fluorescent green poop, because your infant ate half an orange crayon while you were cooking dinner.

They'll bring it in triumphantly. It will greet you with malice, but their voices will hold nothing but joy. Maybe a little confusion. "Look what I found in the trash!" they'll say. "I'm so glad I found this." They'll look at you and tilt their head a little. "Wait. What was it doing in the trash?"

No idea, baby, you'll say, because you'll convince yourself they're asking the same question you're asking.

How did that thing bust loose again?!!

And then you'll wait for them to fall asleep so you can play this game again.

It doesn't matter how many times you try to get rid of this toy. You can wrap it in a towel and turn it off so it can't speak another word and stuff it in the bottom of a bag, under all the table scraps and old dirty diapers and snotty toilet paper, and it will still come back, a little worse for wear (that's a slight understatement. It will resemble The Blob.). You can smash it with a jackhammer, and it will still come back. You can toss it over the fence, way off into the yard of a distant neighbor, because they will surely enjoy it more than you did—it's a minion, after all—and IT WILL STILL COME BACK.

This is a war you will not win. You will have to do what every parent before you has done: accept that this toy is going to be a part of your family for a while.

The next time your kid asks if he can take this keeps-coming-back toy to the children's museum so it can see what it's really like to be a spy, say yes. You might just get lucky and see another kid walking out the doors with it.

Or it might be waiting back at the house when you're all done rejoicing that you'll never have to see it again. Either way, at least you have learned what it means to be resilient in the face of overwhelming obstacles.

The second surprising secret: No matter how much you discard in this whole tidying-up thing, there will still not be enough room for everything.

You're not supposed to look at storage solutions until you've sorted through everything you own and decided whether or not you're keeping it. Don't even think about putting something away until all the discarded stuff has been carted out to the curb. Wait until you've tossed out more than half of what you own, and then try to find space for what's left in your it's-the-same-size house, and watch how it still doesn't fit.

You'll clean out their art supplies. You'll throw away fifteen thousand broken crayons and two hundred dried out markers, and you'll sort all the papers and put them in binders and tuck them all neatly away, and then you'll look at the supplies you have left and realize it's still not going to all fit in the art cabinet where things like this are supposed to go. How in the world did it all fit before? You have no idea. You'll try to throw more away. They don't really need fourteen pencils. Four will do. Still doesn't fit. They don't really need more than one pair of scissors. You don't like it when they use scissors anyway. Still doesn't fit. They don't really need crayons at all. Still doesn't fit.

You realize this is never going to work. There will never be enough space. Because kids have a mysterious multiplying effect on everything except money (too bad).

But you try harder. And you finally cram it all in. "There," you say. "Now everything has a place."

You imagine the whole room clapping, even though you're alone. You pat yourself on the back, because that was hard work, right on up there with rocket science, you'd argue.

And then your kids come home from their grandparents' house with three manila folders full of original artwork, and it looks like a paper plant threw up in your living room again, and there is no kidless weekend in sight where you can make all those drawings of, what is it—a whale? A giant fish? You (surely not)?—disappear so the kids won't notice that not everything they draw is a masterpiece.

Back in the manila folders, you say. Back in the manila folders. And they'll put all those papers back in the manila folders and then you'll have to find a place to put them. Right now, it's the top of your piano, where you have to look at them, out of place, every time you reach down to get a diaper for the baby.

And let's not talk about birthdays and holidays and all the days in between or the days when kids suddenly have enough money to buy what they've always wanted—an oversized Spider-Man toy—

even though you just got done paring down the superhero figurines because they've grown out of them.

How about we just embrace what feels like the truth: there will never be enough room for all the clutter kids come with. And then, if there magically happens to be enough room once every blue moon, we'll be pleasantly surprised.

That's how I like to live my life, anyway.

How Autonomy Ruins Your Tidying Plans

There is something frightening that happens when kids start exercising their independence. They start doing things for themselves. Like washing hands. And getting their own drinks. And making their own food.

I say frightening, because what this inevitably does is it makes it ever more impossible to keep a tidy home. Because they will try to get water from the water filter, and they will accidentally miss the cup and make a puddle on the floor, and they won't clean it up and will forget to tell anyone, and the only way you know about it is when you're coming in to put the laundry in the dryer, and you slip and nearly die, or at least it feels like you almost died, if your heart has anything to say about it. And then you start laughing, because YOU ALMOST DIED and yet you still have to put the load of laundry in the dryer.

And there's the bread they'll try to use for making an after-dinner snack, except they don't pay the least bit of attention to the crumbs they're spreading all over the counter and the butter that was smeared into granite so effectively it was rendered completely invisible, and the only way you'll know about it is when you put the oldest's reading log on the counter, and the grease starts eating all the way through it and you realize it was only a matter of time before you started looking like THAT family.

And then there's the washing hands, which usually results in water staying on too long and somehow not keeping to the boundaries of the sink, because they put their hands right up into the faucet instead of leaving enough space beneath it so water won't splatter everywhere, and there are drops all over the mirror and their shirt. Then, of course, they miss putting the soap on their hands, because they're not very good at aiming (just look at their toilet) and so every time the faucet is turned on for the next five days, it creates a bubble bath right there in the sink, and you'll wonder, briefly, how you might be able to save all that soap and to use in their baths or something, except it's hand soap and good mothers don't use hand soap to wash their kid, except for that one time you were out of body wash and you thought, what the heck, it's all made of the same stuff, and you did and the sensitive 6-year-old's skin broke out and you felt terrible about it. Hypothetically.

Kids come into the world begging for independence. I see it in my infant, who has just started letting go when he's standing anywhere, so eager to stand on his own and start walking that he doesn't care that in the next three seconds he's probably going to fall hard, right on his rump.

And after years of pouring their milk and wiping their noses and dressing them, we start begging for that independence, too (except when our work is gone and then we'll miss it).

The problem is that independence comes with inconvenient spills that will drip all the way down into a cabinet of storage containers, and you'll have to go ahead and wash all eight hundred of them. And it comes with snotty tissues lying around the living room, because he thought that when he used them to wipe his nose, you would throw them all away, not him. And it comes with a pile of clothes heaped in front of the closet, because all these shirts were the ones that "didn't work out" or the ones that were holding on to the shirt he really wanted, and he doesn't have enough time to hang them back up before school starts.

Independence means pencil shavings spread all over the entryway floor, because the 8-year-old was sharpening a pencil and then the 5-year-old tried and accidentally knocked over the entire sharpener and made the shavings go everywhere, and now the infant is happy that there are more things to put in his mouth. Independence means soap all over the bath rug because he's just started taking showers on his own, and sometimes the soap squirt doesn't quite make it in his hand, because he pushes too hard or too soft, but, hey, at least he's using soap, which is more than I can say for the other third graders, judging by the way their classroom smells. Independence means way too many toys taken out, because he couldn't decide what to play with, and he can reach all the toys and unlock the door by himself, and so he just chose, in a moment when you weren't paying attention, to get them all out and save you the trouble. Except he didn't really save you the trouble.

There are some things that will get worse before they get better, and they can usually be linked to independence.

Food messes are the worst.

When they decided they wanted to have oats with milk for a snack, because they enjoy eating raw oats drowned in 2 percent milk (gross), they thought surely they could do this themselves. I was putting the 3-year-old twins down for a nap and was not aware of their plans. They probably could have done it themselves, except they accidentally opened the bulk bag before taking it off the pantry shelf, and the oats spilled everywhere.

Those are the times you'll want to take their independence back. Not really. Because I don't want to be Cinder-Mama. But still. Maybe take it easy on the food, guys.

While it's easier just to do things ourselves, it's good for them to feel efficient in their own worlds. It's also good for them to know that it's okay for them to make those mistakes, and then learn how to clean them up.

As long as it's not oats with milk. Or popcorn (no you cannot eat the seeds). Or water from the Brita filter in the fridge. I've nearly broken my neck three times, and that was just in a day.

There are some things I'd rather do.

How to Make Tidying a Special Event for Kids

Kids will believe anything once.

I know, because the other day we told the kids we were going to have a really fun, cool, relaxing day tidying the house. There were a few groans from the older ones, because they're old enough to know that tidying is work and asking an 8-year-old to lift his finger on the weekend (besides the one that's taking pictures on his camera) is like asking an elephant to lose a little weight. It's a death sentence. Or so they think.

But Husband and I had already decided we were going to make this a game. What kid doesn't like a game? We called it the "Reset Game," because smart parents don't include "tidy" or "clean up" anywhere in the title of a game, and we're nothing if not smart parents. We started playing the Reset Game at 8 a.m., because my kids like to wake up at 6 a.m. on the weekends and burst through our door to tell us they're starving to death. First we explained the rules: Every time they finished "resetting" in one category—say, clearing all the blankets from the floor—they got to ring a bell and draw a reward from a hat.

Rewards were things like ten minutes of jumping on the trampoline or reading for five minutes or choosing a treat from the list of approved ones or an extra story at their story time of choice.

We started out well. The 8-year-old was tasked with carrying all the dining room table chairs from the living room to their proper place, because the boys had used them to build a fort last night and hadn't put them back, since their "legs were tired" and they couldn't walk anymore and especially couldn't drag chairs to their proper place. The 6-year-old took all the blankets they'd brought outside because it was 89 degrees instead of 107 and put them back on their beds. The 5-year-old worked on the 20 billion Battleship pieces spread out on the floor like a whole battalion of white pegs had exploded in our living room. The 3-year-old twins were picking up all the dirty clothes boys had left lying around in their rush to go "jump on the trampoline in their underwear" (which is not allowed, by the way. We're just not always paying close attention, because trying to tame wild animals is exhausting.).

The 8-year-old was the first one finished. He rang the bell, and Husband congratulated him and held out the top hat, where all the rewards were folded up into tiny squares.

"A treat!" he said, his eyes wide and excited, as if he hadn't just inhaled a stack of twelve pancakes drowned in honey. We let him have a bag of Annie's fruit snacks. He crammed them down and was quick to ask what his next task was.

The 5-year-old finished next, which is impressive, considering the piece-count, but he's a pretty exceptional child who has never, ever given up when it comes to a seemingly impossible task. He rang the bell and drew his prize.

"Five minutes on the trampoline!" he said. We sent him out the door. Then the twins and the 6-year-old finished at the same time, and there was a traffic jam at the bell, because the bell stopped working when one of the twins touched it, confirming our diagnosis of those two as The Destroyers (think the opposite of King Midas.

You know how everything turned to gold when King Midas touched it? Everything breaks when the twins touch it. They don't even have to touch it. They only have to look at it.). They all drew their papers, but the twins can't read, so even though I was in the middle of doing the dishes, I had to wipe my hands on my pajama pants and read it for them.

"Treats!" I said. "Everybody got treats." I looked at Husband. He looked at me. Maybe this wasn't such a good idea after all. What if they drew "treat" more than once? How could we take the "treat" squares out if the 5-year-old hadn't yet drawn it? Could we blame the luck of the draw? Did we have to play fair? I had already manipulated the numbers, putting one paper with "treat" on it and thirty-six papers with something else on it, because treat was the most dangerous of them all.

The 8-year-old finished his next task and drew a paper. I didn't even have to guess what his paper said because of the look in his eyes.

"Another treat!" he said.

"Maybe just one now," I said. Tidying the house wasn't worth walls coming down from the boys bouncing off them. I opened up the package of fruit snacks and handed only one out to every boy who drew the treat card. Which was every single one of them every single time. I have no idea how they beat the odds. There were six of each of the six different rewards, and they kept drawing the ONE treat paper I'd put in there. I think one of them must have put an invisible magnet on the back of it so every time they reached in, it jumped into their hand.

We went through five packages of fruit snacks. I knew we'd pay for it later.

A couple of them got to jump on the trampoline, and then the "extra bedtime story" started coming around, after I took the "treat" paper out and stuck it in the bottom of the trash can, so we had five extra bedtime stories that night.

By dinnertime, the boys were bouncy balls, laughing about some kind of game that looked like human bumper cars, except without the seat belts, and we had to pull out the megaphone just to get our voices heard above the roar of hilarity. "Time for dinner!" we said.

"We're not hungry!" they said. Of course they weren't. They ate their weight in fruit snacks.

But our house looked fantastic.

We sat them down anyway, and it was like eating on a rocket ship. The whole table trembled with their shaking legs and arms and faces. Husband and I looked at each other with the same look on our faces.

Never again, we said.

They wouldn't go to bed. I wished for the thousandth time that there was such thing as a tranquilizer gun that would send my boys to sleep the exact moment we said, "Okay, time for lights out." The last one didn't fall asleep until 12:30 a.m. He says he stayed up all night, but I went in to check on them later, and they were all mouth breathing, their bodies twisted like circus freaks, as if they'd just dropped in the middle of an act—which they probably had.

The next time we tried the "Reset Game," the boys were less impressed. They had, after all, figured out the point of the game and weren't quite so thrilled to tidy. It was boring. Hard work. Plus, the treats we were offering this time were grapes. Who would work for grapes? I wouldn't even do that.

    At least I'm raising smart kids.

Why You Shouldn't Aim for Perfection in the Tidying Revolution

There's a good reason why parents shouldn't aim for perfection in their tidying.

It's because your kids are working against you.

Maybe you have perfect little angels who always tidy up after themselves. Maybe your kids never get anything out without asking permission first. Maybe they never bring in the great outdoors that would be better left outdoors, like snails they put in a pantry jar while you're not looking that you will one day, months from now, find sitting on the shelf with the black beans, a whole glass graveyard of innocent snails.

I don't have those kinds of kids. I have the *other* kind. The kind of kids who take out the two hundred building planks and build an amazing contraption complete with twists and turns, and, when finished, are "too tired to clean up." The kind of kid who dumps all five thousand LEGOs out on the table so he can search for that one little piece, disregarding all the pieces falling on the floor that he'll miss in the cleanup. The kind who thinks it would be funny to put a stick under your covers so you'll feel it when you climb into bed tonight (well, at least it wasn't a frog.).

My kids are every day working against me. The last thing in the world they want to have is a clean and tidy home. That's why they leave their shoes in the exact place where they took them off (about five steps from the shoe basket), and that's why they make five thousand paper airplanes out of all their magnificent art and then let them fall where they fall, and that's why they decide, on the very day I've tidied the entire house, that they'd like to make a fort while I'm otherwise occupied with their twin brothers, so they'll bring all the blankets and pillows downstairs and turn over all the chairs to make the largest fort in the history of the world.

My word.

It doesn't take long after I've picked up everything off the floor and vacuumed all the residue that comes in with boys from the outside—maybe about three seconds—for someone to start cutting his brother's dragon picture into a million pieces because someone left the sharp scissors out and he never has the novelty of using those. Or someone decides it would be fun to play a game and gets out Monopoly, with all its paper money and tiny little houses and green hotels and the cards that tell you what to do—except instead of playing, he scatters it all over the living room floor, because it's fun to make a carpet out of game pieces. Or someone thinks it would be funny to decorate that just-cleaned floor with the contents of their art folder, which has reached a paper count of four billion.

I can put my twins in their bedroom for a nap and sit right outside their door, watching them the entire time they're asleep, and when they wake up and I turn on the light (I haven't moved once from my observation post), there are books all over the floor and a mattress streaked with a pen they found somewhere. It's like some crazy voodoo magic, this messiness that kids bring with them wherever they go.

I didn't fully understand it until I had kids of my own. I'm not really a snob when it comes to things like messy houses. But I have always felt the difference of tidiness, even when I was a kid. When I used to go visit my grandmother, who liked to keep stacks of papers and important things in the corners of her house, I could feel the untidiness piling up in my chest. It felt a little like suffocating, like the "things" were making it hard to breathe.

So when I became a parent, I didn't want that to be me. I wanted to own only a few things. I wanted everything to have a place. I wanted to practice simplicity and see my house as a home without a whole lot of "stuff."

I wish I could laugh in that idealistic woman's face today. Because kids.

Kids make toys out of school papers they fold into rectangles and build into a maze. They take grocery lists and shape them into paper airplanes, and you won't be able to find the list until you've already left for the store (and then you'll remember where you saw it). They set up their stuffed animals in an animal hotel because they can't bear to throw away that box your toilet paper came in, and they'll leave the cuttings all over the floor.

They're little Pig-Pens, making a mess of everything I've done. They collect all the junk they could ever possibly want, and I keep throwing it away, and Husband keeps forgetting to take it out to the actual can't-see-through trash bin instead of leaving it in the can-definitely-see-right-through trash bag beside the table so they can find it without even trying and ask me why I threw away their special butterfly masterpiece (it didn't look like a butterfly). I'll keep hiding those renegade toys that don't have a place anymore and they'll keep rediscovering them, hiding them in the holes they dug in the backyard. I'll keep washing the mattress with the pen stains and they'll keep hoarding that pen in a place where I can't find it, and we'll just keep playing this game, over and over, day after day, until I'm carted away to a mental institution, because this is the very definition of insanity, this doing the same thing and expecting different results.

Or.

I'll just give up.

Yeah, that sounds like a much better plan.

You win, kids. Have at it. Live in your pigpen and see if I care. (Stop twitching, eye.)

Always Discard First (Not Your Children. Your Stuff)

Warning: You Must Do the Whole Work of Discarding

This was the summer we were going to get our house in order. This was the summer we were going to get our lives back on track and start feeling like we were in control of something again, instead of all these toys taking up space and making us walk like wary soldiers trying to navigate land mines made of wood and plastic.

"It's our summer of simplification," I told some friends. I felt excited. I love getting rid of things. I love simplifying. I love feeling like I can breathe in my home.

Problem is, I made a huge error in this tidying game. See, the rules explicitly state that you're supposed to discard AS SOON AS you decide what you're throwing out and what you're keeping. You're not supposed to keep those discarded items in a box generically labeled "eventual yard sale," even if the box is hidden in a whole stack of others inside the garage.

But, you know, I wanted to see if our trash might become another's treasure, as they say, so once we were on a roll, pulling things out left and right and labeling them "discard" I had a brilliant idea. "Hey," I said to Husband. "Why don't we set all this stuff aside and have a yard sale?"

"When are we going to have a yard sale?" Husband said. He looked doubtful. Probably because trying to hold a yard sale with kids at home is like setting them loose in a toy store.

"I don't know. We'll see," I said. Details, details.

"The kids will be back tomorrow," he said, still looking doubtful.

"I know," I said. "We'll hide the box."

We both looked at the box. It wasn't overly large. This would be easy.

Let me just tell you now, there is no hiding place that children will not discover. It doesn't matter if there are twenty pounds of your old high school awards on top of the box where their old toys and treasures sit, they will acquire superhuman strength to lift those awards and uncover what's buried beneath.

I probably don't have to mention that my kids found the box. They emptied it, and our hard work was all for naught. I tried convincing them that we could all put on a yard sale, come on, it will be fun, and they could even keep for themselves the money they got from selling their toys. They weren't having it. They played with their old trains intended for 2-year-olds. They played with their old squishy balls they hadn't picked up since they were 18 months old. They played with the toy that says six-to-twelve-months on the unopened box it inhabits.

This was not the only time we'd failed at the discard part of the equation. It was clear that we had what one might call a "discarding breakdown." Typically, what my simplification process looked like is the moment the kids seemed preoccupied and I could manage to sneak around without being spotted, I'd gather up all the junk that needed to be in this day's "discard" box, which would inevitably become too heavy to carry down the stairs safely (I broke a foot falling down the stairs when I was only carrying laundry. I'm "not allowed," according to Husband.). So I'd call for Husband to come get the box, at his earliest convenience.

He would forget about the box.

So I'd work hard all day, sorting things, deciding what to keep, hiding it all from the kids, and then, come bedtime, after they'd burst into our bedroom twenty-five times asking the same question in a different way, they would, because they have powerful observation skills one-twenty-fifth of the time, spot the box with their old things in it.

"My old rabbit!" a boy would say, and off he'd run to tell his brothers, who would come traipsing in to see what treasure they might find that they'd forgotten they even had.

(Hey, kids: there's a reason you've forgotten you have it. You don't even like it anymore. Trust me. You'll leave it out in the backyard, where it will get rained on and grow fungus and start smelling worse than your feet after a day at school.)

To be fair, I did all this discarding during summer break. I could have picked a better time.

The boys would find old books with the covers taken off in a trash bag stuffed away in our closet, put there temporarily until such a time as we had enough energy to take it out to the curb. They went sneaking into the no-kids-allowed garage when we weren't paying attention and came out with the two thousand stuffed animals we'd packed away once, because they have another thousand taking up space already on their beds, and forgot to donate.

And, even after all this, we couldn't find it in us to discard all at once, because by the time we made it to the end of our days, we didn't want to have to go outside our room. Kids are like leeches when they see a parent out of bed. They'll catch us unawares, on our way down stairs and back up, telling us some billion-word story (I don't even know what "the deadly kiss chess move" is) or asking if they should be worried about this cough they have (No. Go to bed.) or wondering what they're having for breakfast in the morning (something you'll probably say you don't like). So we opted to stay put in our room and do the deed later.

"I'll take it out first thing in the morning," Husband would say.

Ten weeks later, it was still in our closet, and kids had taken everything out while our attention was on the 3-year-old twins dumping a can of gasoline in our backyard. Pretty soon you couldn't even tell that I'd done any work at all.

"Hey, I really like this book," the 8-year-old said when he saw a board book that was hardly even a board book at all anymore.

"That book is missing four pages," I said. "You can't even read it. And we can't put it back together."

"Yes, I can," he said. I didn't know if he was saying he could read it or he could put it back together, but he walked out of the room with it before I could clarify.

Once I made the grave mistake of leaving the collection bag in our home library, because I couldn't even lift it, it was so heavy (one of the kids had decided a perfect place to hide a collection of rocks was in one of their chest drawers.). Actually the collection bag itself wasn't strong enough to move, because we use eco-friendly trash bags that decompose while they're waiting to be taken out. So I just let it be, hoping Husband would figure out a way to get it down the stairs without dropping its contents everywhere. The 8-year-old found it and pulled out all his old art work with the food smudges on it, saying he wanted to keep the pages for "memories."

The other day I was working in my cloffice (my closet office, where my sewing machine sits and where once a year I get to sit down and stitch something in peace for seven minutes or so) and the 6-year-old came barging in at exactly the three minute, forty-seven second mark. The first thing he did, even though I was doing something incredibly interesting—making a new cover for a journal—was head straight to the picked-over trash bag still waiting to be taken out. There were only a few broken pencils in it by now.

"Hey," he said. "This is the pencil I got last year for making Star Student."

I looked at what he was holding. It was a short stub of a pencil that looked like any other ordinary yellow pencil, except that there was nothing left to sharpen, and the tip was broken. I shook my head. "Go ahead," I said. "If it makes you happy, take it."

He walked out with a smile that could dim the sun.

Visualize Your Perfect Home. Now Add Sweaty Socks All Over the Floor.

One of the oft-repeated mantras of tidying experts, when offering advice on how a person might achieve a once-and-for-all kind of tidying is to visualize the destination. Visualize the nice, clean, streamlined home that you want to live in and then take the necessary steps to get it.

I did this. I saw open floors with no toys making my walking path turn into an unexpected booby trap. I saw couches with no random toys peering out from beneath them. I saw art supplies that were put back in the right cabinet and papers that made it to all their proper places instead of spread over every possible table and counter surface.

I saw organization.

And then I had more than one kid.

The dream for a perfectly clean and perfectly tidy house fades a little more every day you live with children. Eventually it will be so opaque that you won't even be able to remember what tidy once looked like.

We all know the power of visualization exercises. Science has proven their importance. But what visualization of an always-tidy home does for me is it makes me feel like that picture is way too far from the reality I know. I start, instead, visualizing more toys, crowding all the walking space. I visualize clothes left on the floor, no matter how many hampers I have lying around and how many times I tell them to pick up those clothes or how often I take that quarter from their allowance because if they're not going to do it themselves, they're going to have to pay a maid.

There's a different dream when it comes to tidying a home where children live. My dream is that these toys won't get a mind of their own and overtake the whole house.

We tried really hard, for a long time after we had our first son, to keep our house simple and uncluttered. We wanted minimal toys and enough art supplies for him to use at a single sitting, and we wanted a place for everything.

His first birthday rolled around, and we encouraged people to buy books and art supplies rather than toys. No one listened. And then he turned two, and we encouraged them to buy experiences or gift cards to frozen yogurt shops or stores, and no one listened. Now he's 8, and he wants all the Pokemon cards in the world for his ninth birthday. We didn't even try to suggest anything this time.

I blame it mostly on the grandparents.

See, we don't buy many toys, mostly because we know exactly how many we have. We don't buy those tear-out-the-paper journals, either, because we know what kids will do when they're given perforation. We don't buy puzzles with a million pieces because kids.

But grandparents don't listen. Not even when we tell them our boys would prefer going on a trip to the frozen yogurt shop, or somewhere they can order their own food. They just get so much joy out of giving those toys that kids will play with for two hours and then decide they're not interested in anymore, because someone left a permanent marker on the counter, too close to the edge, and this is a much more entertaining toy.

The last birthday we had in our house, we decided to make the gigantic leap to LEGOs. Big mistake. Big, big mistake. We now have a hundred billion LEGOs that never get put away properly, because "I want to save this to show my brothers when they come back inside," or "I want you to take a picture of it so I can show my teacher" or "I don't want to break this."

Everyone who came to the party brought more LEGOs, which is really generous of them, don't get me wrong. It's just that we were under the grand illusion that we could keep these LEGO sets nice and neat by telling the kids they could only open one package at a time and put it together, and only then could they move on to the next package. Everyone knows LEGOs don't work like that.

Every one of those boxes was opened and dumped in the middle of our dining room table, where people had just eaten cake (some of them clearly more experienced at it than others). Those LEGOs seemed to like the smears of cream cheese frosting. I don't blame them, of course. I worked hard on that icing.

It's not just birthdays, either. It's Christmas and Thanksgiving and every time they visit the grandparents who take them to McDonalds and let them come home with those cheap toys that break fifteen seconds into playing with them but, somehow, still end up in our toy box.

So, yeah, I visualized a house that had no toys visible to the people living inside it. I visualized a house with toys in themed collections, and not too many. I visualized a house where all the toys were put away in their places and hidden from view, as if no kids even lived here.

But now I'm not so sure.

The thing is, we can work toward a house that has no toys showing in the important places, but it won't look like a house that's lived in. We can work toward a house that has all the toys perfectly put away every night before dinner, but then we miss out on the fun of playing a cleanup game with all of us on the floor, together.

So I've come a long way. Now I visualize a home that looks lived in, a home where a few stray Hot Wheels wait to be discovered in the gap between the couch and the floor, a home where kids feel free to explore the miracle of play.

There. That feels more like it.

The One Question You Should Never Ask Children

The summer of simplification began in June, and we were off running. Sprinting, really, and I didn't plan on slowing down anytime soon. I moved from category to category, just like those tidying experts recommend.

But there was a hurdle waiting that I didn't expect.

Stuffed animals.

My kids have thousands of them. I'm not really sure how it happened. I know we didn't buy them all. I know the boys get a small allowance every month, and they're usually spending that allowance on these little wide-eyed animals called Beanie Boos, from the local Hobby Lobby store. I know that they have no concept of having too many or whether or not they should stop buying. I know kids are always drawn to "stuffies" that can seem like real friends.

For a while, we tried to encourage them all to pick different Beanie Boos, because there's a whole collection of them—owls, foxes, dogs, cats, penguins, tigers, every animal you could possibly imagine, and they all wanted them all. Problem is, that means we currently have ten thousand stuffed animals, and now we have to give away nine thousand, nine hundred of them, because there's nowhere to sleep anymore, unless we're talking about a mattress made of fluffy animals who stare at you without blinking.

So we thought we'd go through each and every stuffed animal, asking the owner of it, "Does he bring you joy?"

I picked up a raggedy dog with an ear missing.

"Who does this belong to?" I said.

"Me, me, me!" said my 5-year-old. "That's Little Valentino."

"Does he bring you joy?" I said, thinking the masculine ending on Valentino meant he was a boy.

The 5-year-old giggled. "Little Valentino's a girl," he said.

"Okay," I said. "Does *she* bring you joy?" I already knew what the answer would be.

"Yes!" he said, grabbing Valentino away from me.

"Even with a missing ear?" I said.

"Yes!" he said again, and gave the dog a big kiss. "I love Little Valentino."

"Where's his other ear?" I said.

My boy shrugged. "I don't know," he said.

I managed not to shake my head, though, to be honest, it bothers me immensely that my son wants to keep an old raggedy stuffed animal with a missing ear and a gaping hole where you can see the fluff inside, because I know that fluff is, one day, going to end up on the floor. I'm guessing it will happen in the 3-year-old twins' room.

But what can you do when a boy loves a stuffed animal?

I held up another dog that only had stuffing in its bottom half now, because she'd been well loved. I hadn't seen her around for a while.

"Huh. Where did Sissy come from?" I said.

"I found her in the garage," the 8-year-old said. "I don't know why she was there."

In the garage, meaning she must have been cleaned out in the last stuffed-animal reduction six months ago. Which means there were probably others that had been in that trash bag. Which also means these were stuffed animals that weren't missed until they were found.

I went through the motions, my voice a tad less excited. "Does Sissy bring you joy?" I said. (A word to the novices: Stuffed animals with names are always going to bring joy.)

"Yes," the 8-year-old said. "That's the stuffed animal I slept with when I was two. Remember?"

Of course I remember. But I don't like to remember, because that makes me want to keep it, too, and we're trying to *reduce* here.

"Are you going to sleep with her?" I said. "Would you even miss her?"

"Yes!" he said, and tossed her up to his bed.

I sighed.

"Okay," I said, hoping I'd have a little luck with the next one. "Whose is this?" I held up a snake that didn't even have any stuffing left. It looked like a furry green tie. It was missing an eye and the tail had a giant hole in it.

"Mine!" the 6-year-old said.

"I've never even seen this before," I said. "Where did it come from?"

He shrugged. "I don't know," he said. "But I love it." Of course he does.

He took it from me and wrapped his arms around it in a hard squeeze, except there was nothing to hug but himself. It was just a piece of material, draped over his arms.

We were getting nowhere.

We ended that exercise without getting rid of a single stuffed animal. The boys piled up all those dogs and snakes and owls on their beds like long-lost friends, and I was no closer to reducing them than I had been when I started. I'd wasted two hours keeping what I'd set out to get rid of.

This experience taught me that kids probably shouldn't be involved in the tidying-up process, especially during the throwing-out step. Because everything brings joy. The markers that don't work anymore bring joy. The roller skates with a missing wheel bring joy. Even the piece of paper with one scribble on it brings joy.

"But it's a drawing the twins did, Mama," the 8-year-old said, when he saw me walking this particular drawing toward the trash bag. "Do you really want to throw away a drawing that one of the twins did?"

Why, yes. Yes I do, when it's a drawing of absolutely NOTHING.

"If you don't want to keep it, then I will," he said. He looked angry that I could even suggest throwing some piece of art away.

Well, he's not drowning in the papers, so…

The bath toys that are all mildewed because they've been hiding underneath the cabinet since the first one was born in 2006 bring joy. The paper airplane he made out of an old report card brings joy, even though it's been crumpled and re-made and doesn't fly anymore. Those socks with the heel-sized hole in them bring joy, because "I wore these that time I learned how to ride the scooter."

(And how do they remember these things? I can't even remember what I wore yesterday. I'm just kidding. Black workout pants, like I wear every other day.)

So the moral of this story is "don't involve the kids."

Two months later, when the kids started school, I snuck into their rooms the first day and bagged up some of the looking-worse-for-wear stuffed animals that I never see them carry around or hear them mention. It's been ten days, and they haven't said a thing about missing them. This could be because their room looks like a clothes volcano erupted inside it, but that's neither here nor there. I think we're mostly good.

Bye bye, stuffed animals. I win.

One Time-Saving Tidying Secret You Won't Want to Miss

How about I let you in on a secret that will save you so much time: When we take on a tidying, throwing-out project, we cannot—I repeat, cannot—let our children know about it, or, worse, witness it.

You probably already know this, but in case you don't, you've been warned.

The problem, you see, is that when kids notice you're cleaning out a room, stacking up all those "beloved" stuffed animals they don't use anymore or clearing out space in their closet for the next year's clothes or setting all those toys they never play with anymore in the pile labeled "garage sale" (Wait. I don't do that anymore. I get rid of it.) or throwing away the puzzles missing half their pieces that will, by all accurate estimations, never be found, they freak out. And I mean FREAK OUT.

But then, if you take heed of the danger that is letting kids know you're on a tidying rampage and keep it a secret operation, the problem then becomes, how is this possible?

Kids are like ninjas, breaking into a locked and barricaded room to look through and dismantle a discard pile you don't even remember leaving there. They sneak into your bedroom at night while you're already sleeping, as if they can sense what's in that trash bag stashed in your closet, and they'll pull out all those books with missing pages and torn covers. They can slip into a room while you're looking the other direction and undo your we're-throwing-all-this-away work in 2.5 seconds, and the whole room will look like a crayon volcano exploded.

It's impossible to keep kids from seeing and sensing. In fact, I'm convinced they have a sixth sense called "What my parents are throwing away today."

They can sense when a parent gets a wild hair and convinces herself that she could probably organize this whole room in a morning, while they're drawing happily at the table (never happens. It's just wishful thinking.). Kids inherently know when something of theirs is being discussed, even if it's silently in your own head. They will barge into a room that you were sure you locked behind you, at the least opportune moment, when you're standing in the middle of the room with that "art piece" they did at the kitchen table without asking to use paper, and they will see the trash bag open and ready in front of your feet, and they will ask you, quite frankly, what you're doing. And you will either have to lie, or you will have to tell them you're keeping this forever and ever (and they will remember).

Kids will do everything they can to thwart your discarding efforts.

Even when you think you've got it figured out, they will beat you to the winner's line (disheartening, yes. But at least you're not the only parent to be beaten by your kids).

This one time we put all kinds of papers in a trash bag, and I cleared out all the old toothbrushes I caught one of the boys using to plunge a toilet with a present in it, and Husband took it directly out to the trash bin in front of the house, where it waited for the trash man to come by first thing in the morning, and when we woke up, those nasty toothbrushes magically reappeared in the cup designated to hold them, waiting for half-asleep children to paint their teeth with sewage.

Another night the 8-year-old was tasked with taking out the trash, and he found the little baby socks that are for a baby younger than three months (his youngest brother was five months old already). He pulled them out, of course, asking, "Why are these here? Why did you throw them away instead of donating them?" The answer is because I know what kind of socks they are. Crappy. They wouldn't stay on our baby's feet, and so I didn't want to give them to any other parents who would feel just as frustrated as I do about socks that don't work. Then he challenged me to think about how they could be reused. I taped them over his mouth. Perfect.

It doesn't matter how many locks a door has on it. It doesn't matter how dark it is inside a room. It doesn't matter how immediate that trash pick-up is, kids will know.

Trust me. They know everything.

But here are some things you can do, if you can't possibly keep your discarding project from your kids:

1. When one of your child's friends comes over, send something you want to discard home with them. It's like a hostess gift, but in reverse. "Please, take these old socks. You'll probably throw them in your own trash, because they don't work at all, but it's the thought that counts, right?" Encourage your kids to give things away (just not to my kids). Then it's someone else's problem. And, bonus, it develops a giving heart in your kid, and gets them used to parting with things they love, like nasty toothbrushes that apparently still

really mean a lot to them.

2. Wrap a grandparent's gift with the art paper that only has one squiggly line on it. That way you can tell your kids you're just using their works of art to bring joy to another person. You're not throwing it away. Grandma is.

3. Tell them you will save those tennis shoes they wore in kindergarten with the soles flapping off for their firstborn son, and then, when they have their firstborn son and he asks where those old tennis shoes are (because he'll remember), pretend there was a fire he never knew about.

4. Wrap a teacher gift with old worksheets. If your kids are anything like mine, they get offended when you try to recycle their school worksheets, even though every day they bring home fifty each (I have three in school. That's one hundred fifty worksheets every single day). But if you reuse that worksheet to wrap a gift inside, it won't look cheap. It will look artsy (just consult Pinterest if you don't believe me). And then it will be on the teacher for throwing away their worksheet. (This isn't foolproof, of course. If you have a persistently creative child like my 8-year-old, he will come back home with the worksheets, because he wants to "keep them for himself," which means he wants me to keep them for him. I promise, baby, you're not going to miss this Reading Comprehension sheet about green toads when you're 18.)

5. Try to make an art piece out of all those scribble drawings, and massively fail. That's okay. You can always give it away to a grandparent, who is probably responsible for giving them all those art supplies that are coming out your ears anyway. Pay them back the best way you know how: with paper.

The Life-Changing Madness of Tidying Up After Children

6. Have a stuffed-animal-burying service. For the ones that are looking really bad and aren't the least bit fixable, dig a hole in the backyard and put them in it (just don't dig a deep hole, because of what comes later). Have a memorial service, where you talk about what the stuffed animal meant to you. When the kid is sleeping, dig the stuffed animal back up and immediately take it to your friend's trash bin down the road. They'll never think to look there (or so we like to tell ourselves). When they try to dig the stuffed animal back up because they "just want to check on him" let them. And then explain about dust to dust and ashes to ashes. It would make a great science lesson on decomposition.

If all else fails, just sell your house and tell your kids you promised the new owners all the toys would come with it. I know it's not entirely true…or maybe it is. There's a new revolutionary idea. You're welcome.

If You're Mad At Your Family, It Could Be Your Messy House

Some tidying experts say that if you're mad at your family, the house could be the cause.

Well, yeah. I've been mad for eight years, which also happens to be how long I've been a parent.

I feel angry, because no matter how many times I tell the 8-year-old to make sure his shorts and T-shirt get in the laundry when he's finished taking his shower, in the three minutes between rinsing out his hair and returning to the library for story time, he's already forgotten. I feel angry that no matter how many drills we've done with the put-the-backpack-on-the-hook-after-school-and-also-all-the-lunch-stuff-in-the-sink, the 6-year-old still races out to play as soon as he's deposited his still-packed backpack on the living room couch. I feel angry that no matter how many times they've practiced cleaning up cars and the tracks they like to build for those cars, the 3-year-old twins will still forget that "I too tired" is not a good excuse for not cleaning up. It only means they'll get to take their naps early.

How could a parent not feel angry about all that?

So many days I feel like all I ever do is nag. "Don't forget to put your plate in the sink before you leave." "Make sure you put that book back where it goes when you're finished." "Hey. Button your pants." Flush the toilet, pick up those pencils, clean up the art supplies, put your shoes away, don't leave a banana peel on the floor, don't leave your blanket in the hallway, are you done with this cup, brush your teeth, hang up that coat.

We have a multitude of laundry baskets strategically placed around our home, but my sons still forget where every single one of them is OR they leave their clothes two inches away from the basket, with the smallest corner actually touching the basket—the ultimate laziness. I'm a mom, not a maid. I don't want to spend the rest of my life, or the best part of my life, cleaning up after the negligent, thankyouverymuch. That's why I try to teach them things like How to Wash Dishes and The Proper Way to Wipe Off a Counter and Where the Trash Should Go. But I also don't want to be the constant nag who only talks to her children when they've left their empty oatmeal bowl on the table.

I try so hard to be unaffected by the lack of cleaning initiative in my house. I've done little experiments with this, looking at the mess the twins have made with their crayons and casually delivering the news, "Okay, boys. Time to clean up. Pick up all the crayons that are on the floor and the table and inside your pants, and let's make this room neat and clean!"

Inevitably, one of them will lie down on the floor and say, "My legs are tired."

"Fortunately you don't need your legs to pick up crayons," I'll say, my blood pressure moving up a point or two.

"Yes I do," he says.

"Well, if your legs are too tired I suppose you could take your nap early," I say.

To which, he will emphatically reply, "No!"

Here is where I typically revert to my 3-year-old self, because the state of the house affects me, whether I try not to let it or I just give up that trying. When there is a mess in a room, I feel the mess in my soul, and I don't like feeling that mess. So I will usually pontificate about how they won't be able to use the crayons tomorrow, because that's the consequence we've established in our house, and I talk about how sad they'll be when they want to color and I'll have to say, "Remember how you didn't clean up the crayons yesterday? That means you don't get to color today."

They will argue with me the whole time, because this is what 3-year-olds do, and they're much more practiced (or maybe just more annoying) at it than I am.

The truth is, I can try all I want to be unaffected by the state of my house, but it will affect me. I feel uptight when I look around a space that looks more like a site where billions of miniature cars fell from the sky than a room. I feel stressed when there is more paper floor than tile floor. I feel angry when I just did laundry, and the boys are now walking all over the clean clothes they never put away.

Which means my emotions are generally one of those three in this household of children.

At the same time, I'm tired of this tidying battle. It's a battle that will blacken our souls, I think. It's one that will leave us bloody and frustrated and most likely in worse shape than we might have been had we just decided, once and for all, that this was going to be a semi-messy house.

My 8-year-old is one of the most creative people I've ever met. Usually his grandest ideas come about five minutes before he's supposed to go to bed. Which means, while I'm feeding the baby and

Husband is wrestling twins back into bed, he takes the opportunity to staple forty sheets of paper together and bring twelve markers to his room so he can start on his baby brother's ABC book.

"What is something of my baby brother's that starts with an E?" he said the other night, when he'd pulled it out and, along with it, a thousand other papers that, apparently, got caught in the swipe of his hand.

"Um, I don't know," I said. "What are you doing?"

"Writing in my baby brother's book," he said.

"It's time for bed, though," I said.

"I just want to do this one thing," he said.

There it is, and there it remains—a room of scattered art supplies I just finished tidying.

Maddening. That's what living with children is. It's maddening.

And the best part of it is that all this losing, all this tidying-that-doesn't-really-tidy, all this pushing and pulling and giving up is remaking me into someone new, someone better, because it's always the hardest things in life that shape us the most. Turns out, in my years of sharing a home with boys, I've gotten pretty good at doing things twice and exercising patience and, mostly, letting go.

But if you leave your shoes in the living room so I can trip over them and pull a muscle in my backside one more time…

What to Do When Your Kid Says, 'You Keep This.'

We're clearing out the 8-year-old's old art supply case, because it's all broken and there's even a clasp missing, which means it doesn't close all the way, which means he can no longer carry it around like it's intended to be carried around, which means I'm just about to put it in the trash, since there's not much we can do for it now that it has been completely and utterly disfigured, and he stops me.

He grabs the trash bag from my hands and peers inside. "What are you doing?" he says.

"Throwing this away," I say, taking the trash bag back.

"I don't want you to throw it away," he says.

"But you can't use it anymore. Everything's already collapsing. You can't carry it. You can't even store your art supplies here, because someone thought it would be funny to kick a hole in it."

"That wasn't me," he says.

"Yeah, okay," I say.

"But it was my first art supply case," he says.

We stare at each other. My eyes probably say, *So?* And his most definitely say, *Please?*

"Well, I guess if you can find a place for it, you can keep it," I say.

"No, you keep it," he says.

To which I reply a long and lengthy silence. I don't even know what to say. I only know that I didn't sign up to be the one he pawns everything off to. But this is the child who will go through all those art papers and bemoan the fact that he doesn't have any more room in his designated art folder that we've given them all for expressly this purpose—so the millions of art papers don't start pushing us out of house and home—and then he will say those cursed words: You keep it.

There are variations to this, of course. There's "I made this for you," or "This was supposed to be for your birthday," (three years ago) or the one that gets me the worst, "Don't you want to remember how I drew a fox when I was only 5?"

Most of the time, because the drawings don't really make much sense to me—and if he doesn't want to keep it, I probably don't want to keep it, either—I'll sneak it into the recycling bin while he's sleeping.

But lately it's gotten worse, because it's not just the art papers anymore. They're nothing compared to the well-loved stuffed animals and the old toys and birthday cards and such. I think he's caught on that we're discarding.

I constantly remind myself that it's good for our kids to learn that they don't have to keep everything. Maybe they'll one day use that paper on which they connected two lines together and not much more, but chances are they probably won't, because who can even tell what it is? He draws much better now, and you know what? I keep the things that are full of personality that I don't think we'd be able to quite capture somewhere else. I keep enough.

When we're cleaning out kids' stuff, they get to learn perspective and know that it's okay to get rid of "stuff." The last thing I want to do is turn my kids into hoarders who have to keep everything just because they made it once upon a time. So I do my best to help them see what's worth keeping and what we can give ourselves permission to throw away.

Usually it looks a little something like this:

Me: I'm going to put this in the trash.

6-year-old: Why?

Me: Because it's from when you were, like, two.

6-year-old: And I didn't know how to draw.

Me: Well, it's not that you didn't know how to draw. It's just that you draw much better now. And I have some 2-year-old drawings already. I don't need more.

6-year-old: Yeah, I do draw much better now. See? [Holds up a picture of a vampire that he'll address to me and put on my standing desk so I can look at it while I'm writing and remember that if I don't churn out a certain number of words today, someone is going to come suck my blood. Probably the mosquito that seems to have taken up residence in my room. How long do mosquitos live? This one's at least two years old.]

It gets a little more complicated with the 3-year-olds.

Me: Anything you tear out of the coloring book is going to be thrown away. Papers need to stay in the books.

3-year-old [cue the sound of magnificent tearing]: But, Mama, I made this for you.

Me: Okay, I'm sorry, baby. I'm just going to throw it away. That's the rule. We have to have rules about paper because—

3-year-old: But I colored it.

Me: I know. I appreciate that. It's just that we have a rule about paper.

3-year-old: But I colored it for you, Mama!

Me:

3-year-old:

Me: The whole picture is pink.

3-year-old: I know.

[I walk to the recycling and put it in the trash. Other 3-year-old tattles on me, and then I have a screaming, implacable 3-year-old on my hands. Two, after one of them hits the other because the other called him loud.]

It gets even more complicated with the strong-willed 8-year-old who has a bit of hoarding in his blood. He's the kid who will scour the trash cans and pull out an old, disgusting baby pacifier and claim he can make a yo-yo out of it. And he will, too.

A home that is too filled with "stuff" is not a very happy home.

So what it really boils down to is perspective. As adults, we have the perspective that kids lack. We know that they'll just replace that one piece of paper they drew on two years ago with thirty pieces of paper tomorrow. We know they won't even miss it once it's gone; it's just the pleasure of seeing it when they forgot they had it.

It's not easy to help them see that right now.

But what would be even harder is trying to walk around in a house flooded by a sea of paper and toys and things. I'm terrified of that.

So in the cleaning out, we're teaching them the value of opening space for all those greater masterpieces they'll produce in time or those more entertaining toys or just empty space. It's good for them to gain perspective. My kids operate under the assumption that they have to keep everything, that they will need it all later, and I'm here to help them realize they don't and won't.

Cleaning out all those old things they don't need anymore is good practice for my kids when they get older.

Just don't ask me to get rid of those stories I wrote in first grade. I already refuse.

On the Impossibility of Throwing out Baby Clothes

Our youngest son is now seven months old. That means I've had to clean out two whole sizes of clothes, because he is our last, and our garage is tired of holding boxes of clothes to pass down, which it's been doing for eight years.

The clothes are still in relatively good condition. I think it's because we sort of gave up around the middle, when the twins were born. We figured if they had a diaper on, that was accomplishment enough for a day. Dressing them was just overkill. So most of those packed-away infant clothes were only worn, at most, four times.

But there is a box I trip over every morning at 4:55 a.m., when I stumble out of bed and into the bathroom to put my eyes in so I can actually see. It's a box of clothes I was saving for my sister-in-law, because they were surely having a boy. Except they weren't, and so now I have to find someone else to gift with a bunch of boy clothes, because we're not keeping them. I mean, I've already pulled out probably five outfits I remember each of my boys wearing when they were infants, because I couldn't bear to part with those early memories (They were how small?). But this box, it's a big box. And we really don't have room for it.

I know it probably sounds silly to the less sentimentally-inclined, but I don't want to give those clothes away to some random person I don't know. There's something special about the infant clothes all folded up nice and neat, and maybe the people in my life don't want their newborn to wear clothes that have been worn by six sons (it was technically only four, like I said.), but honestly, I have a really hard time donating them to some random charity.

Maybe it's because I don't want to lose the connection with those clothes after all these years. I'm probably being too nostalgic about it all. It's probably ridiculous and weird. Yeah, well, what's new.

It's just imperative, in my opinion, that the clothes go to someone I know. I want to know the baby who is wearing them. I don't have to see him every day or even every month or week. I just want to know that the baby is wearing my sons' clothes.

Part of this irrational need is that this is the last time. This is the last time my boys will ever wear any of these clothes, and they're so full of memories it feels like getting rid of them also erases those memories. I know that's not true. The memories will remain even when the clothes are out of sight, but that's hard to convince a heart when hands are going through the box again. See? Here's the little jumpsuit the oldest wore when he laughed out loud for the first time, and it was the most magical sound I had ever heard in all my life. Here's the shirt the second son wore for our first family pictures as a family of four, and, yes, I know I have the evidence of the picture, but there's something about the fiber and the way it feels when I touch it and the way memory hangs in its smell. Here's the jacket the third son wore the night we had Thanksgiving with our family, and there are the matching fedora hats the twins wore when they looked like little old-men gangsters, and there's the boat onesie our youngest wore when he came home from the hospital, even though it swallowed him whole.

Tidying experts would tell me it's silly to hang on to these unnecessary things. They have no practical value. No one will ever wear them again, unless they're dressing their leg up as a baby for Halloween. They have no purpose, except to remind a mama of how small her babies once were.

I think this is purpose enough. Because it's true that the days are long but the years are short, and I've just turned around and suddenly he's eight or driving or graduating, and I want to be able to remember that first laugh and that first family picture when we moved from a party of three to a party of four, and I want to remember that first Thanksgiving when he was around and wanted to eat our food but couldn't yet. I want to remember that he once fit into the crook of my arm.

I know I'll remember all that without the clothes. But there's something that happens to memory the further away we are from it. It starts to fade. We start to forget how very small they were and how it felt like just a few seconds ago they couldn't even use their words and yesterday they were happy just to sit in their Bumbo seats and smile so broadly at us simply because we'd walked into the room (now we're the worst parent ever upon walking into a room.).

This whole box holds memories for me. I remember the outfit the first one wore home, and I remember which outfits we bought for the second son, because he was born in a completely different season that didn't need winter jackets, and I remember which ones we got as gifts and how that sweater hat was the cutest thing ever on all their heads, but the simple reality is that I will not be able to keep them all. I will have to let them go, as I will have to one day let my boys go.

I've had my first practice doing it. Another sister-in-law is having a boy, and I've delivered all the earliest clothes to her. And now, some other baby will make new memories in those old clothes. Those fibers will hold a lot of joy and wonder and love.

I never thought I'd miss a box I tripped over every morning.

There's a Reason You Should Leave Mementos for Last

There are some things that are much harder to throw away than others, and this is why, tidying experts say, we should save those things for last.

These mementoes are different for every parents. Some parents like to keep their kids' teeth, while that makes me throw up a little in my mouth. Some parents like to keep their kids' hair cuttings in a little envelope or sealed container, to remember how soft and fine it was once upon a time. Some parents like to keep old clothes or a stuffed animal that's been slobbered to death or a pair of "first steps" shoes.

Me, I have trouble throwing away art work or anything that has my kid's handwriting on it, with a little added personality.

This means I have a bin in my closet where I put all the amazing stuff (which is really anything at all they create, although I've gotten better at differentiating between what's really amazing and what's just a normal part of my child's day—mainly because they create six billion pieces of art a day). That bin is bursting at the seams.

In it is the piece of paper on which one boy wrote a little essay so full of personality and voice that my writer's heart jumped for joy that an 8-year-old could find his voice so early (now if he could just keep it). In it is the drawing the 6-year-old did of the grinning cat with a curling tail that's simply amazing, if I do say so myself. In it are the spider-like people the 3-year-old twins like to draw and call "Mama and Daddy." In it is the first piece of paper where the 5-year-old wrote his name in all caps just after he turned 4. In it are all the "graphic novels" my 8-year-old has written in the last year, because I think he'll be glad I kept them someday (my mom did the same for me, and I am forever grateful.).

These things are incredibly hard to throw out.

So I've been leaving the bin alone, letting it continue to grow and expand. It's quite easy to ignore this bin, because it's tucked away in my closet, and, also, I don't have the time or energy or emotional capacity right now to sort through its treasures. So much of it is sentimental, because one thing we can't do with time is turn it back, and that's a sobering reality when we're faced with the choice of "throw this away or keep it forever?" Will I be glad I kept that drawing of the fox he did before he could even write his name? Will I be thankful I kept that word problem that had fractions and used his family as the slicing-up-a-pizza example? Will I know exactly why I kept those drawings that look nothing like portraits?

I like to think I will.

I'll go through that bin, eventually, but I don't know that I'll get rid of much of what's in it. Because, for me, those papers dig up memories. And when he's starting his last day of school, the *last* last day, I think I'll be glad that I can pull out the sheet he filled out in kindergarten that says he wants to be a movie producer when he graduates high school and compare it to what he actually wants to be now. I think I'll be glad that I can show him the drawings he used to do up in his bed at night, when we were no longer paying attention because as soon as our heads hit the pillow we were already asleep, so we can talk about how far he's come in his art development. I think I'll be glad I kept this bin that takes up arts and crafts space in my closet, because it holds pieces of them.

Every one of those papers brings some kind of joy. They remind me of a crazy-yet-simple time, when my kids were little and they were content with just a piece of paper and a pencil and a day didn't even contain the word "bored." It reminds me of a time when they were adding six plus three instead of doing complicated calculus equations on three sheets of paper. It reminds me of a time when they used to leave love notes wherever they wrote them.

They'll be glad, too. Because in that bin is also something that they will want and need someday: the encouragement and blessing notes the members of our family wrote for them every time they celebrated a birthday or started a new year of school. That's something valuable, too.

Or maybe they'll just think it's cheesy that their mom kept all of this junk. Either way, they'll still have to go through it, which means they'll have to see what I saw: that they are amazingly creative, full of potential, and deeply loved.

The Best Way to Tidy is By Category (Or How to Drive Yourself Insane)

The Mystery (and Frustration) of the Lone Sock

I bought a collection of workout socks a few months ago. They're bright colors like blue and pink and purple, and so soft it feels like I'm leaping on air when I'm doing my squat jumps during my interval training workouts.

Recently one of them went missing.

I don't understand this mysterious phenomenon. I don't know where these socks go. I know that when my boys play out on the trampoline, they take their socks with them and then, after a few minutes of "slippy-slide jumping" they take them off and throw them all over the yard, but I'm not 5. My socks get where they're supposed to go, which is the laundry hamper as soon as I'm done with them.

From the laundry hamper, they are sorted into piles in the middle of my dining room floor, and from there they're carried to the wash room, which is a short twenty steps from their piles. But they don't have to be carried in my arms and risk being dropped. They're rolled in a rolling laundry basket with a screwy wheel (because this is life). They're put straight into the washer and transferred straight into the dryer. There are no holes in the floor of our home. As far as I know, there are no holes in my washer or dryer, either. These socks are really bright. I would have noticed if I'd dropped one.

So what happened to the other pink one? Well, that's anyone's guess. Maybe there's a magical portal in the middle of the dryer that steals the socks it wants to steal and leaves the match because whoever runs the portal really loved that old TV show Punk'D. Maybe the sock will one day unexplainably reappear when we've gotten rid of the mate. Maybe someone in the world needed it more than I did.

But when I finish folding laundry and there's a missing sock, I'm always faced with an important conundrum: Should I keep the lone sock, or do I get rid of it?

The problem is, if I got rid of every lone sock, my boys wouldn't have any left in their drawers. Every one of their socks is a lone sock, and they've gotten good at pairing them up anyway. We started a lost-and-found basket just for socks, because all those lone ones were getting out of hand, and if there's one thing I hate, it's one sock sitting in a drawer where there should be two.

The boys don't mind. They'll mix and match any time. The other day the 6-year-old came down wearing a shin-high Christmas sock on one foot and a black ankle sock on the other. He was, of course, wearing shorts.

"You're really going to wear those?" I said, eyeing his bottom half.

He looked down, too. "Yeah," he said. "Why not?"

Why not, indeed. Well, there would be several reasons in my book, but for a 6-year-old boy, who really cares? Certainly not him.

The reason he's stuck wearing only one shin-high Christmas sock is because the last time I did laundry, the mate disappeared. I specifically remember putting both of them in the dryer, and only one of them came back out, because the other sailed away to the North pole, where it really belongs. I'm sure its mate will join it soon, but I won't tell the 6-year-old that. He loves those socks. He cried when he lost the first one, and I had to check the dryer vent to see if maybe, impossibly, it had gotten sucked up in there somehow. I checked behind the dryer, to see if there was, improbably, a hole in the back wall. I checked all around the floor to make sure someone hadn't opened the door and let it fall out and then kicked it behind all the junk that seems to think it's found a home in my laundry room. There was no second sock.

Seems the 6-year-old has solved that problem, though, so I don't have to worry myself about it any longer. But I do have a pink sock in my drawer that is missing its mate.

Little by little by little, all the socks are disappearing. We spend more money on socks than we do on winter clothes for our kids. Well, I guess that's not saying much. We live in Texas, where the average temperature is 150 degrees.

Sometimes I find the socks. Sometimes they're hidden quite proficiently in our backyard weeds, because some little boy decided he wanted to play outside on the grass that's really hay without the inconvenience of socks and then, when it was time to come back in, he forgot he'd taken them off and tossed them to the wind. Sometimes I find them under couches, where a school boy got home and couldn't wait to get out of his sweaty, stinky shoes and commenced *throwing* both the shoes and the socks off, rather than taking them off like a sane person would do, and they lay where they landed, drying out in the fan's breeze. Hey. At least they're dry by the time I touch them. There's little worse than a wad of wet socks.

Sometimes I even find the missing socks on stuffed animals, because apparently Sully's feet got cold last night. It's no wonder they don't have enough socks to make it through a whole week. They outfitted seventeen Beanie Boos.

So back to my lone sock. It's been three months since the mate went missing, but I still don't want to throw it away, because I just know it's going to turn up somewhere. Even now, it's probably pushed into a corner where I can't see it, and when I get around to cleaning behind the furniture, I'll find it. And, besides, another one, this one bright purple, has joined it in the back of my drawer. So, if worse comes to worst, I'll be able to pair them together. Don't judge me. These workout socks aren't cheap.

I'm holding out for one of these days, though. One of these days the purples and pinks will be reunited.

"You should probably just toss them," Husband says tonight, peering over my shoulder into the drawer. "You have enough."

"They're good socks, though," I say.

"You're going to wear them when they don't match?" He looks at me with his eyebrows raised, as if this is the most doubtful thing in the world.

And I can't say a word, because, well, he knows me. Of course I don't wear mismatched socks. I'm not 5.

But you better believe those socks aren't moving from the back of my drawer anytime soon.

If You Don't Wear It, Toss It: On Lingerie

In my tidying efforts, I finally made it to the top drawer of my dresser, which is where all the old lingerie went after we had our first baby and none of it fit anymore. I haven't opened this drawer in eight years.

"Hey," Husband said, looking over my shoulder. "What's that?"

I pulled out some pieces, laid them out on the bed. "Just some old lingerie," I said.

"I remember those," he said, picking up a couple that made it on our honeymoon, in little white bags he would pick every evening. "Good memories."

Good memories, but not good fits anymore, unfortunately. So I started to put them in the trash bag that was waiting right in front of me.

"Wait. What are you doing?" he said.

"Throwing them away," I said. "They don't fit, and no one wants hand-me-down lingerie. That's disgusting."

"How about you keep them?" Husband said.

"How about I don't?" I said. They didn't fit. And, besides, these were younger years, back when it was exciting to wear something that was cut out in all the right places. I live in a house with boys. I don't wear lingerie anymore.

Husband pulled them all back out of the trash and laid them in my drawer. "I want you to keep them," he said.

But what Husband didn't understand is that there was a criteria for keeping everything. We were supposed to be going through everything in our house and holding it in our hands and asking ourselves whether it brought joy. Did this little tiny piece of mesh fabric bring me joy? No, it just reminded me of how far I've come since we got married. Six babies later, my body is a little fleshier than it used to be.

Do I really want to have a reminder of that sitting in my top drawer? Nope.

"Just for a year," Husband said. "If you don't use it after that year, you can throw it away."

Now. I know for a fact that I am not going to use this lingerie. Anything that tiny is not going to stretch itself onto this body anytime soon. Those were the good old days, back when we were young and tight and excited about the new life we were building together. And while we're still young (mostly) and (somewhat) tight and excited about the life we have built and continue to build together, there are some things that passed right out with a season.

Like lacy white brassieres that don't cover a whole lot.

It's not too difficult, in my mind, to reason lingerie out of my drawers. They belonged to yesteryear. Now I don't sleep in something like this because I live in a house of boys, and sometimes they need me in the middle of the night. Sometimes they burst into our room unannounced, and I don't want to scar them for the rest of their lives if they do. I still remember standing at the bathroom door when my grandmother asked me for a towel, gaping in shock that she'd opened the door completely naked, and I was a *girl*. That's not the kind of scar I want my boys to have, which is why, when I have the privilege of showering, I lock the door behind me. It's why, if I have forgotten my towel and my boys are the only ones home, I drip dry, knowing very well that the extra eight minutes will cost me a few pounds of strawberries (it's worth it). That's why lingerie is something of the past.

Also, why would I want to put clothes on just to take them off? Those are valuable minutes we're wasting, minutes when kids could wander and come knocking and spoil the whole mood.

But you know what? Who am I to dash a man's dreams? I kept it. I folded it and arranged it in my top drawer, for another day or for never (most likely), and smiled. "Okay," I said. "We'll see if I've used it after a year."

It would take me a thousand years to squeeze into these tiny things, but I didn't tell him that. I just shut the drawer and turned to him and put my arms around him. "Thanks for making me see reason," I said.

He laughed, because he knows sarcasm when he hears it. I married a smart man.

He pulled me back onto the bed and kissed me and we…

Fell asleep.

Because kids.

Why I Can't Possibly Unpack My Purse Every Day

There's this school of thought that says in order to keep a house tidy, you must always put everything back in its place. I agree with this school of thought, even if it is simplistic and wildly idealistic when you're a parent. Kids, as we've already established, have the astounding ability to tear the whole house apart in less than three seconds of entering a room. They don't even have to be *in* a room to destroy it, trust me.

But, still, we try to do that putting-everything-back-in-its place. We do the best we can.

And then there's this even more radical school of thought that says, if you *really* want to maintain the tidiness, you must also do things like store your shower things outside the shower and unpack your wallets and purses every single evening, once you're done with them.

Okay. I get it. I really do. My purse has been holding three Hot Wheels for five months now, and at least that time frame might have been shortened if I'd actually been cleaning out my purse every time I walked through the door.

It's just that when I walk through the door, I'm within seconds of getting bombarded by boy bodies flying at me from every direction because I was gone for such a long time and they all missed me and this is what they did in school and they got eggs at the grocery store and their daddy let them have a little treat because they helped fill the cart. They're already pulling me toward the table, because dinner is ready and we eat promptly at 5:30 p.m., because if our house doesn't keep to a schedule it will be midnight before Husband and I get to put our feet up.

There's no time to unpack a purse and hang it where it goes.

But it only takes five minutes, you say.

To which I say: Do you know what can happen in a house of six boys in "only five minutes?"

Let's see. There was the time I locked myself in the bathroom for less than five minutes, for a little space and quiet, and I came back out to chalk drawings all over the walls, because the 3-year-old twins had found the chalk stash (at least it was chalk. That's relatively easy to clean compared to the permanent markers they typically use.). There was the time I accidentally fell asleep for four minutes, because we had a new baby and I was so tired, and I woke up to find a 3-year-old running with the scissors his brothers had left out in a place where he could reach. There was the time I went upstairs to dump some laundry on the bed to fold later, and I came back down to the whole house smelling like gasoline, because the 3-year-old twins figured out how to pick a lock and drag out the gas can in Husband's shed.

So, no, I don't really have five minutes to spare. I'd like to keep my house standing for now.

Not only that, but it would take me more than five minutes to empty this purse. Do you know what I have in here? There are all the receipts from last month's Target visits that I still haven't recorded in the ledger. There is an old wad of gum that ate the paper it was wrapped in, which I threw in here the time the 6-year-old said he didn't want it anymore and almost tossed it into the middle of a parking lot, where my shoe would find it, like it always does. There are the random toys—the Hot Wheels, a couple of LEGO pieces from who knows what creation, some kind of wooden block, some Monopoly money.

Those are just the things I can identify.

Then there are the things I can't, like these crumbs from something that might resemble crackers—the problem being that my kids don't eat crackers. I don't eat crackers. There's what looks like a mangled paper clip, all rusty and brown. There are nail clippers, which are easy to identify but confounding to look upon, because who in the world would put disgusting nail clippers that still have a piece of toenail stuck to them IN MY PURSE?

At any rate, this is going to take a whole lot longer than five minutes.

But if you do it this time, it won't take as long next time, you say.

False. Do you know how many times a kid will go digging in a mom's purse, even though she tells him to leave it alone? There are days when I don't leave the house for a week, because I'm a closet hermit, and the next time I pull my purse down from its place, it's so heavy I can't lift it past my ankles, and it's easy to identify the culprit: Captain America, Iron Man, and Robin. I don't know how they got there. I don't really want to know.

This purse seems to attract all the things my boys don't put away. I'm convinced it's some elaborate prank, all the boys whispering the plot to see what Mama will do this time. It's not funny, boys. Stop.

At one point, I even had the luxury of a dirty sock in my purse. My billfold smelled like rotten Fritos for weeks.

My purse is also a repository for all the things my kids don't want to hold. This would be things like school papers, stuffed animals, dirty coins they found on the ground. It has all sorts of hidden compartments, and when my boys see them empty, they think they might as well use them.

So I guess I'll just take my kisses at the door and head straight for the dinner table, because this time is precious, and I'd rather spend it here than emptying out a purse.

The Endless Art of Shelving Books

Not long ago Husband and I sorted through all of our books, trying to decide whether we still wanted them all, because we had so many. Thousands of them. I had read somewhere that freeing up your house of all the intellectual knowledge that's in books and only keeping the ones you'd want to read again or the ones that actually mean something to you or that you'll use for something, could free up space in your mind for the intellectual. I didn't know if I believed it.

So we decided to try it. I sorted through all the kids' books first. We have so many picture books that it takes nine bookshelves in our home library to hold them all. And they're all precious and dear, because there are some I remember reading to my firstborn son and others that we used for some cute baby pictures, when he sat in the middle of a makeshift library and opened every book, always curious about the words within. And some of them were books we'd read with our newborn twins, who stayed in neonatal intensive care for twenty-one days. Some of them were books I'd packed in my hospital bag with the second and third son. Some of them were gifted to the last born son.

Some of them are beautiful, some of them are funny, some are old classics I remember having as a child.

It was one of the hardest things I've ever done.

I pulled out all the books, which included quite an impressive number of middle grade novels, since that's my favorite kind to read, and laid them out on the floor. I couldn't get myself out of the corner I'd put myself in after that, but I was determined to sort through them all. Just that room alone took three hours. I would pick every single book up, look at the cover, listen to it speak to me, and set it in either a discard pile or a put-back-on-the-shelf pile. On and on through the thousands of books, and I had a discard pile of only about fifty and a put-back-on-the-shelf pile of, still, thousands.

I had to do better than this.

It's just that it was so hard to part with those books and the stories I loved. I ended up keeping all of the ones I'd stacked in the put-back-on-the-shelf pile, even though I sorted through them all again, because they were each special in their own ways. Some of them had to be thrown away for practical purposes—because kids had destroyed them—and I recorded their titles on a sheet of paper, knowing the most deeply loved books had ended up in the trash, irreparably damaged. They'd been read a billion times. My kids would miss them.

It's not easy to get rid of books when you're a book lover like me. I read picture books and middle grade novels and easy readers, because I always want to know what books bring my boys joy and help them feel more like reading and push them further along in the journey of life.

I wasn't even remotely finished yet, but I still had the library in our bedroom office, so I knew I would probably get rid of quite a few of those books. Those, after all, had been collected during twelve years of marriage, and some of them we had never even read and probably never would, because life is busy. And kids.

So I pulled them down one bookshelf at a time and sorted through them all. I threw out old novels I probably wouldn't read again. Some of them were duplicate copies, because I'd kept some anthologies from college, and you really only need one copy of the Complete Works of William Shakespeare. Some of them I'd gotten as gifts and was never really interested in them anyway. This discard pile was much easier to grow, because I hadn't cleaned out these books since college, and who needs an old media law book and a British lit anthology with only excerpts of the great novels? Some of the books I had grown beyond. Some of the books I rediscovered and put back on my shelf, because I knew they would help me with specific writing techniques that I hadn't considered in quite a while.

I cleaned off a whole seven shelves of books and had that much room for other things. I got rid of about three hundred books (and still have probably a thousand more, at least, in just our bedroom library—I told you, we have a lot of books).

But because it was so difficult for me to get rid of books—especially the ones I hadn't even read yet even though I'd had them for six or more years, I could better understand my boys' reluctance to get rid of anything. The thing is, when you really love something like I love books and they love their art, it can feel awful to decide what to keep and what to toss, because each piece is precious. It didn't matter that some of the books had never been read and I might never read them, I just love books. It didn't matter that his picture from when he was 4 years old wasn't anything compared to the picture he can draw now, he wanted to keep it because he loves art.

In the end, though, I discarded. And in the end, they, too, will have to discard. Because if we were to keep everything in the world just because we love what it is, not even for its individual value but for its value as a whole, there would be no room in our house to live.

Husband came sauntering into the bedroom while I was sorting through our books.

"You're going to throw out some books?" he said. He looked very doubtful, probably because I've never cleaned out our books. In fact, it is much more likely that I would be adding that many books to the shelves that were already overfilled. Which is actually why I cleared off those seven shelves—to make some space for the new books I want to get. Just kidding, babe. That's totally not going to happen, even though I can't stand seeing empty bookshelves.

"Yeah," I said. "It's time."

"I don't think you can get rid of all those."

I started stacking them in a box. "Watch me," I said.

I put the ones that didn't fit inside the gigantic box in a suitcase and watched Husband struggle to carry three loads down the stairs (He won't let me carry anything down the stairs. I'm too graceful.). We drove to Half Price Books, where we made three hundred dollars off my loot.

After which we had a great date night.

That Place Where All the Stray Items Go

Not long ago I tidied up our laundry room. This room also contains a pantry, where kids rummage through bulk items like almonds and walnuts, and, mostly, rolled oats. Every other day, when they're sneaking oats with milk—which sounds really gross to me, by the way, because they're not allowed to get into sugar or honey—they spill some of it. And then don't clean it up. Because none of them did it.

Beside the washer and dryer in this room is a shelf with extra lightbulbs and vitamins (on the very top shelf, where boys can't mistake them for candy—have you tasted those gummy vitamins?) and the reusable grocery store bags that get all messed up twice a week when we venture out to the store and haphazardly grab them from the shelf and just as haphazardly put them back (organization's not our strong point. Mostly because it doesn't really have a point in a home with six kids.). Along with all of these, there is also a shelf that houses vinegar and beeswax and all those hippie supplies that come with making your own personal care items.

But mostly the laundry room is home to random toys.

Because the laundry room has a door, this is the place where most of the odd-and-end toys get stuffed into Mason jars, random superheroes trapped there along with Thomas the Train and Finn McMissile, staring out at all the food they can't have and wondering how long they'll be imprisoned. This typically happens when company comes over, because we just need a really quick fix for our house and then we can let them inside. So the laundry room doesn't just collect all our storable food, it also collects random toys and items that we don't feel like putting away. Clutter is like an understatement when you're talking about this room. It's the place no guests will ever go, because a pantry is private. Who wants to see what a host and hostess eats? Or, in our case, what our kids spill and don't clean up?

Our toys are stored behind the locked door of our garage, because a few years ago we converted our garage into a playroom, thinking this might keep the kids out of toys and prevent extravagant messes no one wants to clean up. We installed a custom lock so that the kids wouldn't be able to break inside without first asking us. (Turns out, kids are much more adept at breaking into places they're not allowed than we even suspected.)

The problem with this arrangement is that, inevitably, when the kids are playing with something and it's time to clean up and they *actually* clean it up, they'll spend all their effort on everything that's visible to them. That means if pieces get pushed under the couch (usually) or thrown behind furniture (every time), it's not going to make it into the designated place for this clean up time. That also means that tomorrow, when a kid is reaching under the couch, because he remembers seeing his old smelly soccer sock there, he'll also find the stray toy that belongs to a package already safe and sound inside our barricaded playroom-that-used-to-be-a-garage.

By then, it's just too much of an effort to unlock the door, get the box or bin down and put that toy where it belongs, because we've already moved on to today's clean-up battles (like the stinky soccer sock).

So what tends to happen is we slip those stray toys into a mason jar that sits on top of the dryer.

A mason jar has turned into five mason jars.

The stray toys live in this translucent home for months.

And because I like my house tidy, without a lot of clutter, this bothers me, even though one might argue that it *is* the laundry room where no one is even going to go. But I know it's there. It's bothersome.

So this one day I decided I was going to work really hard to get everything back where it belonged, because it's really disheartening waking up in the morning thinking, "Today I'm going to master this healthy eating thing" and feeling all the willpower drain from you when you walk into your pantry (which only has healthy stuff in it, by the way) and see all the clutter that belongs somewhere else. That's the reason we eat pizza so much. It's mess-stress eating.

Walking into your pantry and seeing toys imprisoned in five mason jars, begging to be freed, is also disturbing.

And walking into your pantry and not actually being able to walk, because all the stuff on top of the washing machine (that wasn't supposed to be there) is now on the floor, because the washing machine thinks it has to shake violently to get our soiled clothes clean is also annoying. And the machine probably does need to shake that violently to get our clothes clean. But the stray items piled on top of the washing machine don't fare so well in this little dance.

I worked for several hours on this room no one would even see. I even wiped down all the surfaces and made them shine. By the time I was done, nothing was out of place and everything had miraculously found its way back to order, and I felt good about the whole world, because I'd just climbed Mt. Everest, or at least the tidying equivalent.

And then I walked out of the pantry to the forty-three cups lining the countertop, and I remembered that a tidy world was not one I could inhabit. I walked back into the pantry and stayed there for a while.

For the next few days, when I needed to look at a clean and tidy room, I hid away in the pantry. I mean, I was mostly hiding from these little people calling "Mama" every other second, but I was also really proud of my efforts. When Husband found me one day in the middle of the pantry while boys ran wild around the house, he cocked his head and threw out a question.

"What are you doing in here?" he said.

"That's fairly obvious," I said.

He looked around, like he didn't notice anything different.

DIDN'T NOTICE ANYTHING ANY DIFFERENT? Didn't he know how hard I'd worked on this room?

"I'm admiring my work," I said, to give him a hint.

He didn't disappoint. "It does look pretty nice," he said.

I took this to mean he'd noticed the state of the rest of the house. "The kids have been crazy," I said.

"They always are," he said. "You don't have to tell me."

We both looked around the pantry again.

"It is peaceful in here," he said.

"Think we could do it to the whole house?" I said. "Tonight? Maybe right now?"

He held up his hands, like he was surrendering to the laws of entropy, which I suppose we all do when we're parents (Remember high school physics? There shouldn't be such thing as entropy. My house has a bad case of it.).

"Whoa," he said. "Let's not get ahead of ourselves."

And a few days later, I got his point. Because I walked into my clean and tidy pantry, and there were rolled oats all over the floor, and there were jars full of random toys and there were napkins strewn over the rolled oats, like that would hide the spill. I realized then how ridiculous it would be to try to take on an entire house when we were clearly working against six very resistant forces.

So I just stepped over the rolled oats and waited for someone else to clean it up until the day (three months later) I got so tired of seeing a rolled-oats floor (and, also, the baby found them) I went ahead and swept them up myself.

The story of my life.

Sorting Through Miscellany: What Is This?

Tidying experts say that one of the last categories we should tidy is the category called miscellany. This category is reserved for things like pictures and papers and spare change and figurines and anything random that doesn't fit anywhere else.

Miscellany is one of the largest categories you can possibly take on when you're a parent, so I completely understand why I would want to leave this one for dead last. It's going to take the hardest work. It's going to mean pulling out couch cushions (if the kids haven't already taken care of that for me) and seeing all the nastiness that lives underneath. It's going to mean moving the stove, where I specifically remember some marbles rolling into darkness and joining the hardened scrambled egg pieces that hit the floor when the 5-year-old thought it would be a good idea to use the spatula to serve himself fourths. It's going to mean pulling out all the junk from under the beds, and there's no telling what's been living there for way too long.

Here's that library book we paid for a year ago.

Here's a decomposed carrot.

Here are some petrified socks.

Miscellany is also all the art supplies, little tiny papers they've cut into a miniature game for ants, notebooks they've called journals instead of diaries, where they record their daily thoughts (or who farted the loudest at dinner). How do you throw all of that away, but how do you find a place for it all?

The answer is it's not possible to find a place for it all. Which means, in keeping with good tidying etiquette, you're going to have to get rid of some of it.

This won't be easy, mostly because the kids will be holding on to their stuff like they'll die without it. "But we like to play that miniature game, Mama!"

"How can you even see it?"

"Because we're not old."

I'll throw it away on principle. (I'm not old.)

Miscellany also includes stationary, writing materials, and household supplies. All the household supplies you need for babies and children could fill a whole room. Am I really going to have to sort through all the diapers, including the cloth ones, and figure out whether I want to discard them? Am I really going to have to pull out all the body washes and shampoos and soaps and try to figure out if we really need the excess we have (because we're always going to use it, aren't we? Nothing goes to waste in a household with as many children as mine has.)?

Do I really need to gather all the spare change together, when kids will just fling it around the house the next time the phone rings and I dare to answer it?

Well, I was one of the crazy ones. I decided it was at least worth a try. So I gathered all the spare change I could find and stuck it in a jar, which was much fuller than I might have thought, considering no one in my house carries around spare change, and then my 8-year-old spotted the jar and had a little entrepreneurial inspiration.

"Whose is that?" he said.

"No one's," I said. "I'm just collecting all the change that's spread all over the house."

"I'll do it," he said.

And he did, except the spare change didn't make it to the glass jar, it got stuck in his desk drawer. So now there are still pennies and nickels everywhere, because at every opportunity they can find, his younger brothers steal a few more and leave them as their (unconfirmed) evidence all over the house. And no one picks up the pennies anymore, because they've realized they're pretty much useless. I can't even convince them to roll them into something more valuable. So all the pennies stay mashed into the carpet and under the couch cushions and where their baby brother can find them and put them in his mouth for a while to give them a good clean before anybody notices.

We have to save this category for last because we're never going to be finished with it. It will take us forever and ever and ever to get through all the miscellaneous junk lying all over our house, so that "once tidy always tidy" refrain? Doesn't work for parents, because kids not only thrive on collecting random pieces of nothing, but they also look for every opportunity to add another plastic dog they won from a 50-cent machine in a restaurant to our pile of miscellany. They don't care that we don't have a place for it in our house, they only care that they want it, and they have 50 cents to spend.

Kids make their own change out of paper, and then leave it on the table. Would that be miscellany or just trash? They make their own figurines out of the material they sneak from my sewing closet. They make yo-yos out of old pacifiers. They never throw anything away, so this category is massive and never-ending.

We'll never get out of it. It's easier to stop trying.

But, of course, being who I am, I don't stop trying. I clear a space for all the old journals so they have a place on a bookshelf. I make space for the art papers that need to be sorted and the ones the boys have decided they want to keep. The kids are playing along, for now.

I try to forget about that old junk drawer I opened this morning that has some broken clothes pins, twenty pens that don't work, and Spider-Man's missing arm in it. I try to forget that I saw an old milk carton land behind our washing machine, because our recycling bin is on top of it, and it likes to move around a little, shake all the dirt out of the clothes when it's washing. I try not to think about those two bins out in the garage—one that still has all the old tax records from our first year married twelve years ago and the other housing all the old school awards that we don't need anymore. Why would we keep them? Because our grandkids might one day be interested to know that we were once voted Most Likely to Succeed in our senior class?

I don't think they'll care.

Now keeping a house tidy for a whole thirty minutes? That's something that deserves an award.

The Sorting Papers Rule Everyone Should Adopt...Or Not

Papers, papers, everywhere. Clean them up, and they're still there.

My kids want to keep everything. I mean, EVERYTHING.

They want to keep those worksheets from school, where they copied the letter five times (clever!). They want to keep that registration form for an art camp that, let's look at the date here, was *two weeks ago*. They want to keep old Scholastic book order flyers.

My boys come home with so many papers they've thrown our paper sorting method off balance. Even the 3-year-olds come home with a stack of Sunday school papers that makes me want to check them at the door and toss it all before we even leave. I can't even get a break on the weekends, and God knows parents need a break on the weekends. But those are the days my kids will empty a printer tray of its 500 papers so they can do their random one-line-on-the-sheet art. Those are the days they don't pick up those papers and put them where they belong.

The real problem is, when I'm sorting papers for school, because there are so many that come home with three kids in elementary, the boys will find some of their worksheets in the recycling and wonder why in the world I'm not keeping a masterpiece like that, even though it's just a reading comprehension test where he *circled his answers*. He even forgot his name, so the teacher put a big red "-5 No

Name" on it. There is nothing on this paper to indicate that it was his. I'd maybe (probably not) keep it if there were.

I've tried to explain to them that I'm only keeping the masterpieces that show a little bit of their personality, and this one, where they just traced the letter F sixteen times, doesn't really give a window into their personality, unless, of course, you're thinking that wavy line at the top bespeaks the way he hurries through this handwriting practice instead of sitting down to practice neat and tidy letters. Also, this page is the one the 3-year-old twins chewed up when I visited the bathroom, so I can hardly make out anything at all.

And there's the math homework that the 6-year-old pulled out of recycling, because there were scribbles all over it that his 3-year-old brothers did when they found a renegade pencil and decided to go a little crazy on it. We were too lazy to erase those pencil marks and just let him turn it in as is, because, in our house, the dog ate my homework is a valid excuse, except replace "dog" with "twins" and replace "ate" with "destroyed," and then you get a true story. He wanted to keep it, because he got a perfect grade on it, and I get that, I really do, but he's super smart, so he gets a perfect grade on nearly everything, and, also, he's only in first grade, so I keep much more of his writing stuff, which showcases more of his sweet personality. We're not as concerned with grades as we are concerned with our boys developing their personality and feeling free to express it. The papers that prove they are developing their personality and feel free to express it tend to be the ones we keep.

But my boys aren't great at understanding this logic, mostly because they're illogical little human beings. Explaining anything to them is like asking for a megaphone that transforms your voice into Charlie Brown's mother on the phone.

And that's just the school papers. Don't even get me started on the art they do when we're not looking. I find it every morning when I come down to make breakfast and pack lunches. It's scattered all over the floor, like we have art-elves or something. There's one with a bunch of squiggly lines drawn all over it, so I think it's probably safe to recycle that one. It looks like someone just wanted to see how many marks he could make before he ran out of room.

One of the 3-year-olds catches me.

"Don't throw that away," he says.

"Why not?" I say. "What is it?"

"A hamburger," he says. He grabs it from my hand. "I want to keep it."

I turn it every which way I can, but I do not see hamburger, and this gets me thinking that maybe there's something wrong with my eyesight, or, at the very least, my imagination, because couldn't I at least *imagine* that this was a hamburger? Nope. It's just a bunch of black squiggly lines that don't even make a circle.

Hamburger fail. That's what it is. I toss it in the recycling when he's not looking.

Anyway, the paper usually goes into the recycling bin when all the boys aren't looking, because they have an attention span of about four seconds when there's food around (about 1.3 seconds when that food is pizza), and they'll forget about that masterpiece they drew as soon as the bowl of pumpkin spice oatmeal I'm dishing out lands in front of them. Or when they realize they "very need to go potty". Or they start picking their nose.

Clearly, there are much more important things than a silly piece of paper with squiggly lines all over it.

I've tried and tried and tried to get to a place where I can just discard everything, because it would save me so much time—like hours a day—to toss without sorting, but there's always that niggling fear that comes back to bite me: Maybe there really will be a masterpiece in that stack and I'd regret not seeing it when one of the kids asks me about it. And what about those spelling tests where the 8-year-old makes his sentences rhyming poetry instead of stand-alone sentences? Those are way too precious to throw away, because he told me the other day that nobody likes poetry, and yet he's writing it. That's a huge deal.

Maybe I'll just start using the "discard everything" sorting rule for the mail. But you know what? I can't even do that, because what if someone feels sorry for us and mails a coupon for babysitting so we can go out on a date, and then it accidentally gets thrown away with all the junk mail? An offer like that is better than money in the bank. Well, I guess I wouldn't go that far.

I'll just have to keep sorting paper. A few minutes of time every day is worth it for a free date night.

Now, if someone would please get that in the mail…

This is What Happens When You Try to Teach Kids the Art of Folding Clothes

Every week, when I painstakingly do eight loads of laundry and separate all those shirts and shorts and pants and socks (Oh, the socks! They are my nemesis!) into their eight separate piles, and after I put my own clothes away, I let Husband take responsibility for teaching the boys to put their clothes away—because they're boys, after all, and he's a man, and I feel like the lesson is better taught by him, as a man, as their daddy.

It's definitely not because I'm too lazy to put six piles of clothes away.

Husband sometimes does an efficient job of this. The boys are sometimes great about putting their clothes away, and Husband supervises them, because the 3-year-old twins get distracted every other second. But this teaching costs us something, because what inevitably happens to Husband's clothes if, by the third day, he hasn't put them away because he's all burned out of putting clothes away, is they end up all over our bedroom floor. For the first two days, he'll transfer them from the floor to our bed every morning. But that gets old really fast, and he gives up after a while, knowing that he'll probably wear them all anyway. And it's true that the pile gets smaller the further into the week we get, but it doesn't change the fact that there's still a pile of clothes on the floor.

Maybe this wouldn't be so bad if he had my side of the bed,

which looks into our master bathroom. His side, however, looks into the home library. When I'm sitting doing my Silent Reading with the kids, my eye is always caught by the massive mound of clothes smirking out at me.

Most days the boys' clothes will do the same thing Husband's clothes do. Husband will stack them on the stair banister that lines the hallway from our room to their rooms, but they will not stay perfectly perched for long, because as soon as a boy decides he wants to wear his favorite pair of sweat pants, which happen to be at the very bottom of his pile, he'll go digging, and all those clothes will cascade to the floor. Of course, he doesn't have the time to put them back where they came from.

And because everyone else is too lazy (and by everyone else, I mean me) to pick up those clean clothes and put them back in their separate piles on the banister (because I already separated the laundry once, remember?), where they will sit waiting with great hope and anticipation to be put away, what ends up happening to those clothes is that they all get smashed together and kicked clear across the room and thrown on top of another boy's pile, and soon I don't know whose shirt is whose anymore. Forty-five minutes down the drain. Every week.

This week the 5-year-old has been especially tired when I've woken him up for school—not because he's been going to bed late but because early mornings are still hard on 5-year-olds, and he hasn't been in school for long, and the long days are exhausting, too, because he used to take a two-hour nap and now he doesn't get one anymore. So he wakes up already sad that he had to climb out of bed. Add to that the complication of trying to find clothes in this don't-know-whose-is-whose pile, and you have a recipe for a whine that could annoy the world off its axis.

"Mama! Mama! Mama!" There's not even space to answer in all those calls. I just stand at the bottom of the stairs, sweating because there's oatmeal cooking on the stove, and if it burns, we won't have anything for breakfast today. And boys without breakfast...you don't want to uncage that beast.

"Yes, baby?" I say, trying not to let that whining grate too deeply against my skin.

"I can't find any shirts," my 5-year-old says.

"You don't have any shirts in your closet?" I say. I don't want him pawing through that massive pile his daddy set on the banister yesterday after I did laundry. Setting a 5-year-old loose on a pile of clothes is like trying to rake leaves on a windy day. The pile won't stay a pile.

"No," he says. I come up to look, even though this is my sixteenth trip upstairs and the oatmeal is still on the burner. Of course there are no shirts in his closet, because I cleaned out all the shirts he didn't need and left him about fifteen, because the closet was getting too crowded with three boys' clothes in it. And that pile in the hallway? That's a pile that's been accumulating for three weeks now. So. No shirts.

I have to go digging. Meanwhile, the twins are left alone, and the oatmeal is still going (God help the oatmeal!), and who knows what's happening or will happen down there in the unmanned kitchen. I find a shirt and toss it in his direction. It doesn't match his pants, but you know what? I don't even care. My kids can look like orphans if they want to.

You know what I do care about? This pile. Something needs to be done about this pile.

Teaching kids to put away their own clothes would help, of course. And we've tried. We've taught them how to fold, and we've turned our eyes away when they decide their try at folding is "good enough," even though it looks more like a crumble than anything else, because, you know, autonomy and all. They aren't our clothes. We don't have to wear them wrinkled. We watch them put their clothes on hangers and push them into the closet in all the wrong places, but we try to encourage them. ("I love how you just made a new spot for your shirts. But do you think you should maybe stick to the old spot so you can find those shirts when you need them?")

The 5-year-old gets angry when he's trying to put a shirt on a hanger and it's not working so well. The 6-year-old gets frustrated when he can't line up the legs of his pants just so. The 8-year-old doesn't really care how anything looks—he'll wear a shirt that looks more like a crumpled piece of paper because it was "folded" on the floor in a small puddle and has been trampled by six feet over the course of six weeks. He doesn't even care if it's clean (most likely not, judging by that smell)—but he does care that his legs are now hurting from trying to hang up his clothes, so he certainly shouldn't have to do this anymore.

What typically ends up happening when boys are sent to "fold and hang up" their own clothes is they decide, halfway through the process, that they're done with this whole thing, that there are way too many clothes, almost their entire closet, look, and, yeah, it's three weeks of clothes, I get it, but they were the ones who didn't fold and hang it all up three weeks ago.

They give up after a few minutes of "trying," and then they just leave their clothes piles on the floor in their room. The pile then goes through a disturbing evolution. It remains separated for about a day, until the boys are trying to find something to wear the next day of school, and then the piles start socializing with each other and walking to the other side of the room, and before you know it, it's one massive pile leaning in front of their closet.

It's hard to explain to them the importance of doing better, though, because that's exactly what Daddy does. Every night, when they come into our bedroom to kiss us goodnight, they see Daddy's pile and think to themselves, "See? He thinks it's a waste of time, too."

I don't like to nag, but I also don't like walking on a shirted floor.

"You really need to finish teaching the boys how to put away their clothes," I tell Husband that evening. "This trying to find things on the banister or the floor is getting really old."

"I know," Husband says. "It's just that it takes so much less time when I'm the one doing it."

And therein lies our challenge as parents. It takes so much longer to teach kids how to do things, but we can't always do it for them. Sure, it's going to take an up-front investment of probably a few hours (if you have two 3-year-olds who enjoy sword fighting with hangers), but we're going to be glad we did.

At least in another five years or so.

Well maybe.

Probably.

That'll have to do.

What Do Scissors Have to Do With an Untidy Home? Pretty Much Everything.

There is not a day that goes by in my house when boys aren't rummaging around in the art cabinet, pulling out supplies. Sometimes they're searching for the latest coloring book, because they want to scribble on a few of the pages and call it done. Sometimes they're looking for some blank drawing paper, because they just got the idea to create this really interesting-looking snake and now they have to see it for real, instead of just in their heads. Sometimes they're trying to find the pages they stapled yesterday so they could work on the comic book they chose as this year's art project.

And sometimes, in their rummaging, they find the glue and scissors, which, of course, immediately changes their plans.

These are my least-favorite art days.

I don't mind the glue so much. Sure, it gets on hands, which get rubbed all over the glass-top table and make nice little streaks that are really fun to scrape off later. Sure, it gets accidentally dripped on three sheets of paper that then get stacked and stuck together and we have to figure out how to get them apart without ripping a single paper fiber off because the 6-year-old really wants to keep them for his art portfolio. Sure, sometimes the boys lick their fingers clean and won't admit that it tastes maybe a little bit good.

No, the glue doesn't bother me.

It's the scissors that kill me.

This is because my boys use them irresponsibly. What this means is that scissors have been banned from our house more than once, because one of them has decided his bangs are too long and he's just going to cut them himself. He assumes, in making this decision, that his parents are probably never going to take him in for a haircut, and he can surely do this himself without coming out looking like a fool. (Nope. That would be a fail.) Or one of them has used the scissors to satisfy his burning curiosity about what a few cuts might do to a shirt, and now he has a huge hole in an otherwise perfectly fine shirt (why couldn't he experiment on the shirt with permanent stains?). Or one of them decides to cut paper.

Now. It may not seem like paper is all that bad a thing to cut, especially after the hair and the shirt. BUT. The problem with paper is that it gets EVERYWHERE. And I mean everywhere. It's like glitter's first cousin.

Kids don't just like to cut out something normal, like the picture they colored of that minion, and then leave it at that. Oh, no. That would be way too easy for parents. They'll cut out that traced picture of a minion, and then they will cut up that background of the minion into tiny little pieces because they love making a mess they can't possibly clean up, especially once it spills off the table and onto the carpet. And if they're feeling really adventurous and it's your lucky day, they'll glue all those tiny little paper pieces to the table while you're upstairs trying to manage the 3-year-old who refuses to use his legs to walk, because he's making a statement.

My boys get some hair-brained ideas when it comes to scissors. The 8-year-old once decided he was going to cut out some Legend of

Zelda paper dolls that he had drawn. He drew fourteen of them and then left the cutting extras and the scissors out so while I was preparing an elaborate dinner of cold carrots and hummus (it's all I can manage most days), the 3-year-old twins picked up those left-out scissors and went to town on all the leftover paper, the carpet, and each other's hair. They ended up looking like identical orphans.

The 6-year-old once decided he was going to make some confetti for his birthday party, except he didn't tell us until those 3-year-olds (yes, there's a theme in my house) got a hold of the pouch where he'd stashed it and dumped all four billion pieces out onto the living room floor.

The 5-year-old, now, he just likes to practice cutting his coloring pages, which wouldn't be so bad if it weren't twelve coloring pages every day.

Because of all these delightful encounters with scissors, they have now moved to the top shelf of the art cabinet, too high for boys to reach on their own. But that doesn't stop them, of course. Any time Mama or Daddy disappears into the bathroom or is distracted by dinner or a phone call comes through (you wonder why I never answer my phone? Because kids.), they'll drag a chair all the way across the room and stand on it to find this greatest treasure of all treasures. Before we even know what's happening, our house looks more like the Paper Bowl than the Dust Bowl.

It's really hard to tidy a house when you have one hundred billion tiny little pieces of paper all over the floor. Why not use a vacuum cleaner? you might be thinking. These tiny papers are so good at being tiny that a vacuum cleaner doesn't really pick them up, so we mostly have to use our hands, and, go ahead, judge me, I don't really feel like picking confetti out of the carpet when it's time to get dinner on the table. I'm pretty much done.

The other problem is that boys are really good at manipulation. Take this conversation:

Them [whispering because they think I can't hear]: Can you reach the scissors? I need the scissors.

Me [in the other room, preparing dinner]: Oh, no you don't. You are not using the scissors. Don't even think about it.

Them: Aw. I just need to cut this one thing.

Me: What one thing? Come show me. [You know, because I'm a good parent.]

Them: This picture I'm coloring.

Me: That's all you're going to cut?

Them: Yeah.

Me: Alright, just that one thing. [Because maybe we can try again.]

Them: Yay!

Me: Just that one thing. Only that one thing. The one thing, and that's it. Then you put them away. [They don't hear anything unless you say it three times, at least.]

They nod, so maybe we have a win?

Nope. Five minutes later there are four pictures cut out of the coloring book, and the scraps have managed to carpet the floor, and the twins are stealing the scissors from their brothers and trying to show just how much they know about this whole cutting thing and it's all over. It's all over. There is so much to tidy up we can't even.

So. I hide the scissors. The boys find them. I know, because I find the paper scraps and the orange peel scraps and the hair snippets and the mangled toys and everything else they use the scissors to cut.

One of these days. Sometimes I feel like I live for one of these days.

From Where Does All the Spare Change Come? (A Tidying Mystery)

Every time I turn around, there's a penny on the floor.

I usually don't notice it until I'm vacuuming and suddenly the vacuum cleaner won't go an inch further because it's trying to suck up a block of copper, and it's not going to rest until that copper is in its mouth. I turn off the vacuum cleaner and bend down, and, sure enough, there's the culprit: a penny.

I don't even know how these pennies keep finding their way into our house. Who uses pennies anymore? They don't even have a purpose. When I was a kid, I could walk to the corner store down a semi-busy highway, with my mom watching from the porch, and buy ten pieces of Dubble Bubble gum with ten pennies, but today, ten pennies won't buy anything. A hundred of them will hardly buy anything, though my 8-year-old informs me that one hundred pennies will buy one package of fruit snacks in the impulse section at the grocery store.

The 5-year-old came into the kitchen the other day and announced, "Finders, keepers!"

"What's that?" Husband said.

"I found something, and I get to keep it!" he said.

"What did you find?" Husband said.

The 5-year-old's eyes were hugely wide, and his grin matched them, and then he said, "I found a penny!" He held it up for both of us to see, and he was so excited we didn't have the heart to tell him that a penny is pretty much as valuable as a piece of scrap paper, except you can use the scrap paper to capture all the random story ideas that come into your head.

Living in all the corners of my house, near the baseboards—because I haven't cleaned them in more than two years—is all the spare change Husband and I don't even carry, because we only use online banking and credit cards and 21st Century forms of payment. And yet that spare change is mating and having little spare change babies.

It's not unusual that I will be checking behind a couch for some stray toys that boys tossed there because they think it's funny to see me bending over the couch this way and trying to reach as far down as I possibly can, grimacing because I don't want to grab any spiders, and complaining that I still can't reach the stray toys because my arms aren't gorilla-length like Husband's, and I'll see a silver coin winking at me. I wish I were motivated to pick up a quarter like my kids are motivated to pick up their pennies, but I'm just not. Quarters don't mean much to me anymore. Spare change doesn't mean much.

But "Finders, Keepers" has become a mantra in our house. The boys will take off all the cushions on our couch, the way I used to do when I was a kid and people actually carried spare change in their back pockets, where it would spill out into the cushions, and they will, mysteriously, find spare change every time. Who carries around spare change anymore? I remember my step-dad coming home from work and always emptying his pockets into the glass bowl my mom had put on the table beside the door, waiting for him to say we could have it (which he hardly ever did, because we lived out in the country and there was no such thing as an ice cream truck driving down County Road 418). But I have no idea who in my house would be emptying their pockets the same way. Wallets don't even have a place for spare change or dollars anymore, did you know that? Or maybe I just got Husband the cheap version. That little compartment, according to him, is for storing business cards (which are also fast going out of date, because the world is flying miles every minute) and little notes from the boys. Not dollars.

It's true that when my boys get their allowance, it's in cash, so when they pay at a store it's in cash, and they're always handed back their change. Maybe that's where all the spare change is coming from—but I swear we have much more inside than we ever brought in. It's like those quarters and dimes and pennies are multiplying while we're all sleeping.

When the boys go searching for change treasure, it usually ends with kids fighting over who saw it first, because a house that functions under the "Finders, Keepers" rule is one that will hear about it constantly. The 5-year-old will put his penny in a drawer, labelling it his collection drawer, and one day, when he's forgotten where he put his stash of pennies, the 8-year-old will open the drawer, not knowing that his little brother has been collecting all those coins for days and weeks and maybe even months, and he will claim it all.

"It's mine," he'll say. "I found it."

And the little boy who originally hid all the change will argue, and we, of course, will step in to let the finder know that this is not something he can keep, because it was a place picked out intentionally by the owner of that treasure, and before it's all said and done those coins have eaten another ten minutes of my time. I spend so many minutes of my time picking coins up off the floor, and then I spend so many minutes of my time diffusing the arguments that boys inevitably have about whose is whose and where they should put their stuff and what "Finders, Keepers" really means.

All I know is that there is multiplying magic to small change. Maybe dollars don't grow on trees, but small change sure grows in couches. I know, because I cleaned my couches out the other day, and today, when I took the cushions off the couch to test my theory, the space was filled with spare change again. I looked around to see if there was a hidden camera in my living room, because I thought maybe I was on an episode of Parenting Punk'd or something, but I didn't see anything. Maybe the boys are playing some elaborate trick on me. I wouldn't put it past them.

Coins, coins everywhere. There are coins that come spilling out of pockets when little boy jeans are run in the wash (at least it's just coins. I've heard about the marker messes others have.). There are coins in all the junk drawers and even the silverware drawer, where a boy has tried to get it away from his finders, keepers brothers. There are coins in jars and hiding in the fibers of the carpet so the vacuum will find them, and there are even coins smashed into the yard out back, where they'll probably never be found, because Husband hasn't mowed in a month. Our backyard eats a lot of things it shouldn't.

I think I'm going to start playing Finders, Keepers myself. And then Husband and I can fight over whether all the spare change in our house will support a housekeeper or a yard man. Either way, it's a win.

Astounding Stockpiles in Which to Lose Yourself

We've got some astounding stockpiles lying around our house.

There are the clothes, mostly clean except for the way they've been trampled by half a dozen feet a billion times every day. This stockpile can hold up to five weeks of clean laundry, and no one will even notice they're living out of a hallway instead of a closet. You might be wondering, why five weeks? That's how long it takes any of them to realize that maybe they shouldn't have their underwear littering the stairs when their friends come over—at which point they finally put them away.

There are also the piles of dirty clothes in the boys' bathroom, because no one can burden himself with walking the long seven steps to the hamper and putting dirty clothes where they belong. They have much better things to do than make sure their dirty clothes get washed. Like wearing their soccer socks for the seventh day in a row.

There are the books that are way, way too numerous but can't be cleaned out one more time, because I've already done that, and the ones left are the ones that are special and wonderful and beautiful, and what would we do without them? I can't possibly neglect to read my boys *Anne of Green Gables* and *Little House on the Prairie* and *Rebecca*, so I just have to keep them all, and, besides, I'll probably have a granddaughter someday. It's up to me to preserve all these books for her.

And then there are the papers. The papers are in a whole league of their own. There is nothing quite so astounding in our house as our paper piles.

They build so quickly. Three days of not checking the papers in a school boy's folder, and suddenly there's a teetering stockpile. Two minutes of leaving the twins alone while I take a healthy sit-down and there's another paper stockpile, waving at me from the dining room table. One week of feeling lazy and burned out and I won't even be able to locate my kids in all the paper.

Husband and I, for a while, had to rent a storage space for all the papers. This may seem extravagant and really silly, but I kid you not. Our storage facility was mostly full of old tax papers. Neither of us is really sure how many years in back taxes we need to keep for auditing purposes, and we're afraid to throw anything away, lest the IRS comes knocking. Not that we even keep good records. We just have some credit card statements and a whole bin of receipts and the papers we sent out to our tax guy, but, hey, they never said we had to be organized if they ever come peering over our shoulders.

There are bins full of old newspapers where my stories appeared back when I was a reporter. There are the notes from people who appreciated my articles, and there are notes from Husband when we were first dating (which don't exist electronically anymore, because Hotmail doesn't even exist anymore. Just kidding. It does. But it's, like, so 2001.), and there are papers from old college applications and old college essays and old college poems and short stories, because I have to keep it all. There are scrapbooks full of more, you guessed it, papers.

It's so hard to get rid of these old papers.

Not too long ago, we cleaned out that storage space, because we'd finally had enough of paying money *just to keep a bunch of papers,* and the storage owners were telling us we needed to have insurance on the space, so the cost would go up, and we decided that we'd stick all those bins of papers out in our garage, and, piece by piece, clean it out.

It's been sitting there for nine months now.

Our garage used to be a playroom for our children. Now you can hardly walk in it, and it's all because of the papers.

Sometimes I daydream about going on a rampage, sneaking into the garage and dumping everything out without looking at it and bagging it all up to put out front so it's the trash guy's problem now. But then I wonder what I might possibly be missing out on, like maybe some old letters I haven't read in ten years or our old wedding programs back when trendy design wasn't really a thing and they looked like they'd been put together in Microsoft Word. Or maybe those newspaper articles from twelve years ago, even though I've changed my career and will probably never work for a newspaper again, and, anyway, it's all digital now, and all I'd have to do is google my old journalist name, Rachel L. Toalson, to see all the things I've written.

I know all this. I know everything in there is old and that I probably wouldn't miss it if it were to disappear. But the fear is real. It really is. What if there is *SOMETHING*, in all that useless stuff, that would unwittingly be thrown away because I didn't take the time to sort through it, and it was IMPORTANT? What would we do then? How would we possibly survive?

So we keep all those bins that clog up our garage, and children try as best they can to maneuver through the obstacle course to reach the toys that are supposed to remain hidden from them unless a parent is there to help. Unfortunately, we have to send much younger legs in there, because it's a death hazard for anyone taller than four feet and older than 30. What we need is a weekend away from all the kids so we can sort through it all, but the problem is, all I want to do when the grandparents keep the kids for the weekend is sleep.

One time we sent the kids away to the grandparents, and we did clean up the playroom, an entire weekend devoted to the tidying up, and that playroom looked so good we sat in there to watch a movie because you could actually see ten feet in front of you, and, also, you could breathe. But then the kids came home, and it took them all of twenty-three seconds to undo our work, because they were just so excited about a clean playroom and all.

I'm a little embarrassed to admit that our stockpiles don't stay in the garage, though. They've gathered on our kitchen counters and our dining room table (what is a table except a place to put a stack of paper?) and in the corners of our bedroom. I blame it on the billions of school papers our kids bring home every day and the junk mail companies that really, really like us. It's definitely not because we've never mastered the art of filing.

I'm sure we'll get a handle on these papers one of these days. Probably right after we adopt the Just Throw it All Away method of tidying. Which will probably be…never.

I mean, what if there's something important in that stack?

Find a Place For Everything (It Won't Stay There, Of Course)

The Best Trick to Tidying: Make Sure You Designate a Place for Everything

The first rule of tidying, especially when you have children, is to designate a place for everything. And I mean everything. Diapers, diaper bag, clothes, toys, you name it. It needs a place. Clothes in the closet, toys in a cabinet, and papers…well.

Let's not get ahead of ourselves.

I'm here to tell you the real truth of tidying in a house full of children: You can designate a place all day long. You can designate six places for the same thing. But it won't get put back.

I know, because we have some of the easiest places for our boys to put away their stuff. Their clothes, of course, belong in their closet, but they'd rather those clothes belong on the floor or crumpled up in drawers, or, better yet, piled on their bed so they can sleep on them tonight. Their dirty clothes belong in one of four hampers we have strategically located around the house, but I bet you can guess where they actually end up. That's right. Outside. (Totally makes sense. Everybody wants to strip when they get outside, right?) What this means is that when laundry day rolls around, they've got all of one shirt in the laundry and one-half pair of socks (don't ask). And I don't even feel sorry for them, because it also means that come laundry day I'm only doing four loads instead of the usual eight. Win for me.

Except that it's not exactly a win for me, because clothes left outside in the Texas sun and heat are usually clothes that come back in looking like they were expertly tie-dyed, which my sons think is cool. I most definitely don't. That shirt still has to make it through four other boys.

Right before school started this year, Husband spent a whole day painting this wall in our hallway, right by the stairs, installing custom pegs on it where the boys could hang their jackets and backpacks and never have to search for them again. Every single morning their jackets and backpacks are exactly where we expected them to be—not on the hooks—and we're all on a treasure hunt without the directions—or any logic whatsoever. We found a backpack in the refrigerator once. "I must have thought it was my lunchbox. Ha ha."

We have two places for their shoes—one upstairs and one downstairs—and we're searching for shoes every morning, too.

There is a place to put all of this, so why doesn't it get there?

Sometimes I think that's the greatest mystery in a parenting world (besides how you make it through a 3-year-old and, later, a teenager).

The 3-year-old twins, at least, have a semblance of an excuse for their clothes not getting where they belong. We had to pull the dresser out of their room when we caught them climbing on top of it and jumping as high as they could off the top, almost decapitating themselves on their ceiling fan because they're mutants. But they don't get their jackets to their pegs, either. And their shoes never get back in the designated place. Most of the time they're leaving the house with one tennis shoe and one flip flop, because they can't be bothered to do a thing called Look, either.

The Life-Changing Madness of Tidying Up After Children

Husband felt a little discouraged that he'd spent a whole day creating something as awesome as a Backpack and Jacket Wall, but I reminded him it comes with the territory. I reminded him of the hand-lettered chalkboards he made the boys at the beginning of their school years, with their schedules written and drawn out. They don't use those either. They always forget to brush their teeth and they never make their bed and they usually come down to breakfast only half-dressed because they're "starving and will die" if they don't have breakfast right this minute.

That didn't really make him feel any better, though, because he was reminded that now he's actually wasted two, not just one, days of his life on something the boys don't even use.

So the thing about designating a place for all a kid comes with is that kids won't usually put their stuff back in that place. It's not that they're trying to be defiant. It's just that they have much more important things to think about, like how to jump off the trampoline into the greenbelt behind your house without Mama or Daddy seeing (It's not actually possible, kids. You'll impale yourself on a fence post. And I don't really want to be cleaning your guts off the back gate. Also, I'd really, really miss you.). It doesn't matter how many times you remind them that "everything has a place" which is pretty much all I say these days. It doesn't matter that they're the ones spending half an hour looking for their left shoe and if they make us late they'll have time shaved off their designated technology time for the day—they still won't put things where they belong. We've tried pretty much everything.

We've tried subtracting money from their allowance, because if I'm the one picking up their stuff, then they're paying me for maid service. We've tried subtracting time from their daily technology allowance. We've tried sending them to school in their house shoes (the school will send them back home, by the way). Kids don't learn from natural consequences, because, honestly, they really don't care. It's just another day in the neighborhood to them.

The 5-year-old came clomping down the stairs this morning with delightful words: "Well, I guess I can't go to school today."

"Are you sick?" I said.

"No," he said. "I can't find my other shoe."

Well, you know what? That's motivation enough to find the other shoe (not that I'd let him stay home just because he couldn't find his shoe. It's just…the possibility. The 5-year-old at home all day with the 3-year-old twins is like trying to calm down a cat fight while you're dumping the cats in a bath. You get all scratched and bloody, and, trust me, you just don't want to go there).

One thing tidying enthusiasts don't talk about is all the places that kids will find to put their own stuff. Because our mantra in my home is "Everything has a place" and the things that don't have a place are thrown out or given away, the kids have come up with some creative and surprising places to keep their stuff. Like rocks shoved in a drawer that's supposed to hold pencils. Or the stick they found that was as tall as they are and looked like a magical staff, hidden behind a bookshelf. Or the stockpile of broken crayons, spread out under a bed, if you're the twins (which you'll also sneak out of hiding and use to cover your walls with pictures when your mom isn't looking).

Or stuffed-everywhere papers.

We've designated a place for all the art our kids produce. They have binders where they can keep all their favorite pieces, and they have little art folders where they can keep the pieces they don't want to punch holes in. The problem is, no one ever cleans these folders and binders out, and so they get backed up with three billion pieces of art that the kids definitely want to keep, yes, don't ever throw this away. IT'S SO GOOD.

I'm getting a little tired of walking in every other day to see a paper explosion all over the floor, but, hey, at least we don't have to ruin our carpet by actually walking on it.

I'm sure I'll thank them later.

Discard First, and Then We'll Talk

Tidying experts say the first step to getting a handle on your untidy house is clearing out everything you don't need or want. Once you do, they say, you will be miraculously left with only the amount of "stuff" that fits into your space (or less!).

Clearly they've never had to throw a kid's birthday party.

I start feeling anxious about four weeks before another kid's birthday party, because before the Summer of Simplification we had so many toys they were coming out our ears, and, also, people show up with random things that don't even have a place in our house, and we're left with this dilemma: throw the toy away or carve out a new place for it? Annoy the person who gave our boys a gift, or protect our sanity? Because there are only so many places.

One of our family members likes to give the boys thrift store buys on their birthdays, which is fine any other time, but when you have six kids and you're throwing six birthday parties a year, those random gifts can really add up. And then, when you add holidays and special occasions and little trinkets they get for behaving well at school, you're left with a house full of randomness.

I don't like a house full of randomness. And I don't think my kids do, either.

My oldest son has a birthday close to Thanksgiving. When his birthday rolls around, it's been a few months since the last boy's birthday, so family is all ready to go with the coolest presents. It's the time of year when all the new toys are starting to come out, because Christmas is just around the corner. I start feeling intense anxiety when his birthday is creeping up, because I know what birthdays mean: a complete overhaul of our toys. It's required every year. And I didn't really look forward to doing it again.

So I decided to mark up that birthday invitation with some gift ideas. I put things like, "experiences," which are actually proven to produce more happiness than "things" (the kids will thank me later); and art supplies, because you can always use more art supplies, and our boys really enjoy doing art; and books, because I love books and so do my boys and no one can ever, ever have too many books (says the person who just cleared out three hundred of her own. Maybe you can have too many of the *wrong* books, but never too many of the *right* ones).

I actually looked forward to his party, didn't feel anxiety one single time, because I had given everyone the tools they needed to get our boy just the right gift. I had even neatly printed "Please, no toys," on the invitations to his friends, so they would think outside the box and bring something that might promise a little more fun than another Hot Wheels car.

Everyone showed up with a present, and I stacked them where they were supposed to go, right by the ledge labeled "gifts" in pretty letters, and I waited through the food and the cake and the singing, and finally, finally, FINALLY we reached the opening presents part. I was just as excited as my son was.

He unwrapped the first gift. Some Hulk Smash fists that actually made the smashing noise when you pounded them against something (which would most likely be a brother from here on out).

I felt my smile slip a little. I started immediately devising a plan for how we could get rid of those things before someone ended up with a broken nose.

He opened the next one: a collection of bath toys. My face fell a bit more. We'd tried bath toys before. They all ended the same way. Mildewed, slimy, and gross.

One after another, my son unwrapped random toys that had nothing to do with what we already had in our home.

Apparently everyone thought my suggestions were just that: suggestions.

When the party was over and everyone had gone home, we took our boy into the playroom and asked him, one by one, whether he wanted to keep the toys he'd just gotten in place of one of his old toys or whether he wanted to throw the new ones out. We explained that our house doesn't have an infinite amount of space and that we needed to keep things clean and tidy so we could find everything we wanted later.

He was disappointed, but we got through it.

And then there was Christmas and Valentine's Day and Easter and Martin Luther King Jr Day and Columbus Day and every other day the grandparents find excuses to buy them something.

So even though tidying enthusiasts say there is such thing as Once Done, Always Done, if we're watching what we buy and choosing wisely, sometimes parents can't really help what comes into their homes. Because there are boys walking home from school and collecting all the rocks they can find, and there are friends who give them trinkets from the fifty cent machine at school and there are birthday parties.

It doesn't matter if you've combed through every room in your house. This tidying thing will never be good and done—because as soon as there's another birthday, your kid will tell all his friends that he collects Legend of Zelda characters, however he can get them, and that's what he wants for his birthday, even though his mom said he wanted something called "Experiences," but they should just listen to him and not his mom. He knows what he's talking about.

My second son has a birthday coming up. I've made my suggestions, but I doubt anyone will follow them, because we have a track record to prove it. I try to change the suggestions up every time I include them, just to see if anyone's paying any attention. We'll probably end our son's day with some random figurines from Japan, some Spider Man accessories (maybe they'll make noise and spit out spider webs, and we'll be able to put them in the same place we put the Hulk Hands—in the trash), and maybe a new LEGO set, because we don't have enough at all.

After a few more years of this, I'm going to have to institute another rule: Parents field the presents and only give the kids what they'd actually want to get. Because sometimes even the kids don't really know what they want, as proven by the way they play with that new toy for all of half an hour and then forget about it for a year.

Discarding isn't a once-done-forever-done kind of thing when you're a parent. We should just accept the truth now: we'll be doing this the rest of our lives. Or at least until the kids are 13 and the grandparents start giving them gift cards or socks, because they don't know what else to buy them.

I never understood why my mom got so excited every time my brother and sister and I got socks for Christmas. Now I know, Mom.

I'd be excited if my kids had one matching pair in their drawer, too.

On Storage Solutions: Pursue Ultimate Lockdown

The key to storing toys and art supplies and other fun items in the house is ultimate lockdown.

We've already established that it really doesn't matter whether things have a place, because they'll always be left somewhere else. Laundry will not make its way to the hamper. Lightning McQueen will not find his friends in the bin marked "Cars." The soccer ball they're not supposed to have in the house will not find its way back to the backyard and the storage bin waiting for it out there.

When it comes to toys in our house, the consequence for not cleaning up a toy is that the toy is now in timeout and boys don't get to play with it for a certain number of days (longer for toys that have more pieces). I remind them of this consequence calmy, matter-of-factly, when they're especially resistant to picking up anything they've played with, or when they're belligerently claiming they "didn't play with that." Toys in time out are in time out for all boys.

Admittedly, sometimes this isn't fair to the boys. The 3-year-olds clearly don't care about the puzzles getting put in timeout and so won't lift a finger to clean up any one of the sixty-four pieces they threw all over the kitchen for the fun of it. But the 5-year-old loves that dinosaur puzzle, and if he hears it's going into timeout, he'll be the one to pick it up.

So recently we changed this rule. Toys are in time out for the boy who was supposed to clean them up but didn't.

Even so, this is typically how it goes down in the Toalson home:

"Time to clean up," I say.

No response. It's like I haven't even opened my mouth.

"Remember the consequence," I say.

No response.

"If the toys don't get cleaned up, they don't get played with again," I say.

This time one of them will usually call out, "Forever?" even though they know the answer is no.

Sometimes, though, I want to shock them into action with a yes. Because sometimes all it takes is something drastic, like not being able to play with their cars FOREVER, even though they don't really have a concept of what forever is and how long it will be. They're still a little confused about what tomorrow is and what yesterday was. (Frankly, so am I. But in a different way.) The twins, in fact, like to tell people, as soon as they meet them, that "I threw up this morning," even though that was actually four weeks ago. Makes things smooth and perfect when you're walking your older boys into a school with six hundred students in it, and all the moms are looking at you like you're the worst parent ever, get those sick kids away from my kid.

I can't lie to my kids, though, especially when it means following through on that forever consequence, because I could never follow through. I know how much they love these cars. I wouldn't just give them away to some other little boy because they wouldn't clean them up. That wouldn't be fair. So I usually answer, "Maybe," because it's noncommittal.

To which they'll respond with zero activity. They don't really care. So I'll go start a timer, and we start the dance all over again, except this time there's a time limit, so they get to race the clock, SO MUCH FUN! I'll call out how much time is left, and they'll sit there not moving at all, and then the buzzer will sound and all those toys will be taken away indefinitely, because, depending on my mood and the degree of frustration, they never really know how long it's going to be. Most of the time it's three days. Once a month it's a whole week.

The Cleanup Battle usually happens when we've left our older boys downstairs, unsupervised, because we're trying to wrangle the twins into their beds for their nonexistent naps (the twins never sleep), and the older boys apparently, without our supervision, forget the rule in our house that goes like this: Only one thing out at a time.

One of them will take out the LEGOs and one of them will get out Lord of the Rings Risk that I've been trying to throw away for ten years now, because it has a billion tiny pieces and it's the most boring game ever, but Husband won't let me, because he still thinks I'm going to fall in love with playing it someday. The last of them will get out all the coloring books, because he can't decide if he'd rather color in Spider-Man or Star Wars or the Marvel hero book. Definitely not Elmo, though, so he'll toss that one across the couch, where it lands in the middle of his brother's solitaire game of Risk that's not really a game but is just an excuse to dump out the billion tiny pieces and line them up on a board so they all fall down and scatter when Elmo comes crash landing in.

I understand their resistance to cleaning up. It's intimidating to come face to face with such a mess and know that you're the one responsible. That's why we have the rule Only One Thing Out at a

Time, because I only have to look at my bedside table to know how risky it is to have more than one thing out at a time just because we can't decide what to read. My to-read stack is like the Leaning Tower of Pisa.

When it's only forty-three cars scattered everywhere, that seems much more doable. But when it's a billion tiny horseman and ogres and elves and two bins full of three billion LEGO pieces and two hundred twenty-four crayons with sixteen coloring books, it's a lot harder to find that motivation to clean up. I was once stuck in a house with one hundred paper airplanes the oldest made during my "quiet time" break, and I didn't even know where to start. I know how it is to get down eye-level with the mess and not be able to find a single thought in your head, because all you can think is, "I don't know where to start. How do you clean up a mess like this?"

So because we know this about our children, Husband and I have invented a practical technique we might trademark and sell. It's called Ultimate Lockdown.

Basically, you just lock all the toys behind a door so that only the parents can access them and the kids have to ask permission. You rig a closet door with hinges so your twins can't break in and scatter the entire contents of their closet onto the floor (it'll work for about three weeks—and that will be the difference between keeping and losing your sanity. Every day counts when you have twins.). Sure, they have to ask permission to put new clothes on (and, no, they don't need to change every time they wipe their nose on the collar of their shirt), but what does that matter in the grand scheme of a tidy house? You put board games with a million pieces—and puzzles, which multiply faster than you can say *Where'd my house go?*—way up high where they can't reach them (but you have to REALLY put them high—boys can scale walls).

I'm all for free play. In fact, we encourage our kids to play as much as they possibly can in a day. Free play experts would probably ask, "But how do you let them play when their toys are all locked behind doors?" to which I would reply, "It's called The Great Outdoors. Best playscape there is."

Hey, a parent's gotta do what a parent's gotta do. Sometimes that looks like using Ultimate Lockdown to maintain a little sanity.

I sure don't want to see the mess my boys are capable of making with free access to every single toy that creeps into our house.

Would you?

The Only Ingredient You Need for a Disastrous Garage Sale: Children

Every now and then, when Husband and I are done cleaning out things like old toys the kids never play with and stuffed animals they probably don't even realize they still have and clothes that won't fit them anymore and there are no more boys who will ever wear this size, we decide to get a little crazy and have a garage sale.

Having a garage sale when you're a parent is really like broadcasting in banner-fashion to your kids: "Come see all the stuff you forgot you have and try to convince me how much you still want it and will play with it every day for the rest of your life."

More or less.

We have a way to combat this, though. After our kids are tucked snugly in their beds for the night, we will usually sneak everything into our garage, which used to be a playroom but now looks more like an obstacle course of boxes, a treadmill we don't use (actually, that's not true. It's a great place to stack bins of Rachel's Old School Stuff.), and broken art supplies that someone was too lazy to throw away. No one is able to navigate this room unless they've had twenty or more years of practice walking. At least that's what we tell the boys. ("You want to break your leg? Then stay out.")

Our garage sale tactic is to add more junk to the junk pile and convince ourselves that the boys won't come walking in here, because, well, remember the broken leg thing?

Except that sometimes they do come walking in here, and then they find trash bags with some of their old things, like the ABC board book that's been chewed by six sets of teeth and is soaked in immeasurable buckets of slobber and really can't handle anything anymore, especially, apparently, that thing called Picking it Up, because it's disintegrating right now as we're looking at it. This shouldn't even be in the garage sale pile and would likely serve more of a purpose in the trash pile, especially since the 8-year-old has found it and is already saying something like "Are you really going to get rid of this book we all played with when we were babies?"

Yes.

It didn't take the kids long to find our garage sale pile, and now it's like a treasure hunt every other day. But still, because we're persistent, we keep trying. Still we keep piling. Still we keep watching those things we've cleaned out come sneaking right back inside.

I've tried telling my boys they could make money off some of their old toys. They know this drill. Once the oldest made a quarter off a whole bin of super heroes, and he got to buy....a sticker from one of those machines in a restaurant. Oh, wait. No. He couldn't even do that, because they cost 50 cents now. It's too bad inflation didn't hit garage sales.

So, of course, when he learned how little he could buy with those old toys, he decided he'd rather keep them around.

The last time we had a garage sale, Husband sat out front under an umbrella so he didn't cook in the summer sun and made all of forty dollars. That's ten dollars an hour. I made more than that when I was 16.

Maybe the trick is to send the kids out to run it, and then they get to keep all the money they make. Maybe that's where we have it all wrong. The problem is that my kids can hardly count to 100, much less make change.

Garage sales are really kind of a pointless proposition. We save these things because we want to make money off the sale of them, and then we don't really make any money off them, compared to the time and effort it takes to keep kids out of the front yard for five whole hours while we sell all the stuff they've forgotten about and won't ever miss, unless, of course, they see it.

"Want to have a garage sale next weekend?" I said one weekend, after I'd noticed the "garage sale" pile had grown considerably after we cleaned out all the old toys and stuffed animals.

Husband looked at me. "No," he said. "Why would I want to have a garage sale?"

"Because," I said. "You know, we could make a little money off these things we want to get rid of anyway."

"It's not worth our time," he said.

"We could have a date night with the money," I said.

He looked more interested then. He's a sucker for a greasy burger.

So we got everything out and set it all up in the driveway, like items together. I don't know how you run your garage sales, but in ours, nothing is marked. Marking requires too much effort. Potential buyers have to ask us how much an item is, and we'll tell them depending on how much they want it. Value pricing and all.

A whole box of clothes someone else gave us that we don't need? A quarter, please. That box of three hundred movies? Five dollars.

My kids' old superheroes? They're free. Please. Take them.

We generally try to wait for a kidless weekend to have a garage sale, but it doesn't always fall on a neat and pretty weekend, and so sometimes we're having a garage sale out front, and the person who likes meeting people the least (that would be me) sits in the house trying to keep the kids inside on a perfectly sunny, perfectly perfect (except for the thousand-degree heat) summer's day.

"I want to play outside," they'll say.

"You can play outside," I'll say. "In the backyard."

"But I want to ride my scooter," they'll say. Of course they do. They know what's going on, and they especially want to know what's out front, waiting for them.

We have a trampoline, a swing set, a sloped backyard that's perfect for rolling down a hill and crashing into a fence, but all the boys will want to do on a garage sale day is go out front and mosey around the cul-de-sac, waiting for the opportunity when their daddy is occupied with a customer to go stealing another stuffed animal they forgot they had.

I tell them that being outside in the front is dangerous, because there are too many cars coming and going (even though I haven't heard one for an hour), but they say they're big and know how to stay out of the way of cars.

Sigh.

Most of the time I cheat and sit them down to a movie.

The worst part is when the neighborhood garage sale happens. It's typically on the birthday weekend for my second son or on the anniversary weekend for Husband and me, so we rarely take part. In fact, we often forget it's happening until one of our boys comes back in carrying a bright pink bouncy ball that one of the neighbors was selling in a garage sale and decided to just give away because our boys looked like they needed it.

They totally didn't. They have four soccer balls waiting to be kicked in the backyard.

"But this one bounces, Mama," they say when I try to give it back.

To which I say, "Okay," because they'll end up bouncing it over the back fence, where it will end up back at the neighbor's anyway.

Garage sales aren't really my friends, so. Maybe we'll wait until the boys are teenagers to have another one. It's not like we make that much money anyway. We could do better farming out our boys to mow lawns.

If we were wanting to make money, that is.

Anybody need a lawn manicure?

To Succeed in Tidying, Store Everything in the Same Place

There's a school of thought in the decluttering circles that says you shouldn't scatter your storage spaces. In other words, all the shampoo bottles in your house should go in the same place. All the art supplies should go in the same place. All the office products should go in the same place.

These people have never lived with children.

It's true that several months ago I designated a special cabinet in a corner of our dining room as The Art Cabinet. There was a shelf for all their coloring books and workbooks and even some free paper (which, honestly, we really just need to ban, as I've already established elsewhere in this book). The Art Cabinet had shelves for crayons and color pastels and markers and even watercolors, because we're generous parents. It was everything a dear little child could want in his art-pursuit life, all separated into tiny crystal cups I'd inherited from my grandmother but didn't have anything else to do with.

On a daily basis, I find crayons in random places, like their beds (which are a whole twenty-six stair steps away from The Art Cabinet), collected under the couch, and even, strangely enough, in our refrigerator, as if someone was doing art and then decided they were hungry and went to get a snack but left their handprint (a crayon) in the refrigerator—which is really not so very hard to believe in a house like mine.

They should probably be supervised while they're doing art, you say.

Well, yeah, I'll get right on that. The problem is, there are SIX OF THEM.

We're told not to scatter the storage spaces, but kids' toys end up in random places, because they have this one particular characteristic that is much stronger than all the others, and it's this: Scattering things effectively. While they're playing with whatever it is they're playing, they scatter them, like it's some kind of let's-see-how-much-of-the-floor-we-can-cover-with-these-crayons game. And then, when they're tasked with cleaning up, they don't look in ALL the places, just the places that make sense, no matter how many times I've told them they have to look everywhere—like in the toilet and under the coconut oil in the pantry and inside the stove, because I'm about to roast some broccoli, and I really don't want green broccoli to become purple broccoli by mistake.

Kids and looking well are like boys and peeing: you never know what you're gonna get.

"Why is there a Finn McMissile car in my laptop bag?" Husband said one day as he was packing up to leave. He held up the blue car quizzically, as if there were any question why, and it was promptly snatched from his hands by one of the 3-year-olds.

"The same reason I have three of them in my purse," I said, giving a significant look to the boys, because we don't allow pointing in our house. Or blaming.

Husband shook his head.

This is called Life With Children. I hope I'm not killing any dreams for you when I tell you you're definitely not going to be able to keep all your like items in one place. (I like my own art supplies. I'm not a big fan of coloring with crayons that have teeth marks etched in them. So that means I have to keep my art supplies separated from all the rest. Also, who has the time to gather all the shampoo in the house and then, when boys are ready to take their baths, put it back? Not me.).

Kids scatter things like it's their only job on earth, and I guess if you're a kid, that is part of the fun. For example, my twins like to stash Thomas the Train and his friends under the trundle bed where we can't see them, and then, when we've closed their door for nap time, take them out and play (loudly, I might add) with them, as if we can't hear their giggling from where we're working right outside the door (we've been schooled many times in What Happens Behind This Door, so we post up right outside).

Husband once tried to build a barrier underneath our couches to see if that would keep random toys from getting lost in the Under The Couch Black Hole, but all that did was give the boys a challenge —who can hide it behind the barriers where no one will ever see it's here? You don't even want to know what we found when we finally claimed defeat for that less-than-brilliant idea and removed the boards. We'll just say that something was smelling for a very long time, and we thought it was the boys' bathroom.

The truth about storing everything in one place when you're a parent is this: You'll have so many places for storage you won't even remember where the one bin of blocks is by the time they ask for it, because there are twelve of them.

There's also the simple fact that sometimes you *have to* separate things, because you don't want all the treasure—say, Band Aids—in the same place, because one not-on-your-game moment you could turn back around to see two hundred Band Aids stuck to the floor. Impressive, I know. Not so impressive when you're the one who has to clean it up, however.

Don't underestimate the power of a toddler. They will destroy three rolls of toilet paper in two seconds flat, just to see what it looks like when they put it in the sink and turn the water on (or, worse, toss it in the forgot-to-flush toilet).

So you have to spread out those things—some Band Aids here, some Band Aids there. Some toilet paper rolls here, some toilet paper rolls there.

This is the reason we also have two refrigerators in our house—because when you have as many boys as we do, you can't put all your eggs in one basket, as they say. Except it's literal for me. They'll inhale two dozen boiled eggs from the basket in our refrigerator without even blinking an eye, and then we'll have to fumigate our house because of all the sulfuric smells that slip out (or thwack or squeal or pop) when boys eat too many eggs.

All your storage in one space? Do yourself a favor and give up on that pipe dream now.

What to Do with the Washing Supplies

Soap scum: I don't want it.

Tidying experts say you can actually avoid soap scum completely by keeping your bath supplies off the bathroom shelves and in a place that's out of sight and out of mind and out of reach of water (and kids who will empty an entire bottle of eco-friendly lavender soap so they can fill it back up with water and make "homemade hand sanitizer").

I know that this is a good idea. I really do. Because I hate scrubbing off soap scum, and it's really gross when you pick up a bottle of shampoo and it's all slimy, but I wonder if anyone has considered how much effort I'd spend putting those things away.

First of all, I often put things away, out of sight where they can't be seen, and then I forget where I put them, so I would likely spend all my valuable shower time (because there's a shower limit of about five minutes when you have young children) looking for shower supplies. And if I can't find them easily (which is usually the case—because the past me thought it would be a good idea to put them someplace the present me clearly doesn't know about), I'll only have two minutes left, so I just get to step into the shower, rinse off, and step back out, which is not an effective shower, even though my oldest son would disagree.

I know I probably need a system for remembering where my supplies are, but my mind is at capacity right now. The word "system" sounds like "Too hard." Right now it's just easier to keep them in a shower and watch the soap scum build. I'm not the one who cleans the bathrooms anyway. Husband and I agreed on that back when we first married. That agreement cemented when all our children turned out to be boys.

When you're a parent, showers are not an every-day luxury anyway, so when I do have a chance to take one, because the twins have finally fallen asleep for five minutes, I want to be able to shower quickly, and that means everything needs to be where it was the last time I remember taking a shower, which is really hard to say. It's been a few days.

If I put something away out of sight, it's probably going to be very hard to find it again, and those are precious minutes I'm wasting. My 3-year-old twins are masters at sensing when someone is not constantly watching them, even when they're sleeping. We had to install a lock on their door that locks from the outside, because too many initiations into The Midnight Terrorization of 3-Year-Old Twins club made it a necessity. I know it sounds cruel, but when you have a 3-year-old who enjoys wandering at night and somehow breaks into the essential oil cabinet so your house smells like thieves took a bath with peace and calming and lavender and cinnamon, you'll do whatever you can to make them stay put. There is nothing safe or sacred in our house, according to the twins, and most days we have to keep our eyes trained on them constantly, and even then it's hit or miss whether they will try something just for the ridiculous fun of it, BECAUSE THERE ARE TWO OF THEM and they're really good at distracting the parent who's one-on-two and doing all the things they're not supposed to.

But I digress. Showers. They're a luxury when you have kids. That means when I finally have two minutes to spare for one, I want to make sure I don't waste that time looking for supplies or even lifting supplies from their place and putting them in the shower, because my arms already had their strength training workout when one of the 3-year-olds decided he didn't want to take a nap today, and I had to carry him, kicking and screaming, up the stairs.

Plus, I have to be really quiet, because the twins will wake at the drop of a pin on carpet, which means I have to execute my shower with the minimum amount of movement necessary.

It wasn't always like this, of course. Our first three boys slept like little angels, and I never understood why other parents would talk about how they didn't get showers and how they couldn't leave their children unattended for even a second, but now I get it. Even with one of these guys I would feel the necessity of constant supervision.

I'm digressing again. SHOWERS.

My point, if you haven't gotten it already, is this: When I get ready to take a shower, I want all the supplies already there, ready for me. I want to be able to use the quickest bathing strategy I can. Keeping my supplies in the shower affords me that.

Also, when the supplies are kept on the shelves of a shower that will make noise if I happen to fall asleep on the couch for a 10-minute-power nap, they are much safer from curious hands than those stashed in a cabinet that only whispers in comparison. (Before you tell me about toddler locks on cabinet doors, let me just tell you about my twins. Wait. I already did.) Trust me when I say, a whole bottle of eco-friendly soap, dumped onto a tile floor, will take hours to clean up, because every time you wipe the floor, more suds bubble. It's like your entire floor is made of bubbles. You'll want to flood the bathroom before it's all over. And maybe you will.

And because you'll probably never want to deal with that kind of catastrophe again, you may as well put your shower stuff on the highest shelf you can possibly find and leave it there, soap scum and all.

The Most Common Battlegrounds for Entropy

We've talked about the law of entropy. Not considering your children, the law of entropy is the biggest reason you can't keep a tidy house.

Husband and I don't always have the time to put all the out-of-place items back where they go, so we designate a holding spot. In my house, that holding spot is the banister that lines our stairs.

On this banister, we'll put things like the plates from that time we ordered in at 10 p.m. so the kids wouldn't smell the food and turn into beggars like they normally do. We put things like pens and markers that the 3-year-olds have an astounding ability to find. We put things like clean clothes after we've done all the laundry and it took all our energy just to turn the shirts and pants right side out and search for sock pairs.

("Do they make monogrammed socks?" Husband said after this week's laundry.

"Well, if they did, we wouldn't want them," I said. "The boys manage to lose their socks two minutes after buying a brand new package. Look at all these stray pairs."

"At least then there would be a one-in-twelve chance that we'd find a match," Husband said.)

This banister also sees the action of stray toys that somehow made it back upstairs when we weren't looking, stacks of books that are out of place and we're just too lazy to put back on the shelf, mugs

Husband is growing unintentional science projects in (Materials: coffee cup and coffee. Just let it sit for a month, and see what you get).

But the problem is, when we leave something out, no matter how tiny it is, it's always going to attract ALL THE OTHER THINGS.

It's like, *hey, guys, why don't you all come hang out at my party? Obviously, that's what those doofuses intended, or else they would have put me away.* And all the other things listen and obey, unlike my children.

Before I know it, the whole banister is covered in randomness, and what I really want to do is bag it all up, except most of it is articles of clothing, and I know someone else will be wearing that in another year, and I don't want to buy a new wardrobe for boy number three.

When we cleaned off the coffee table in my bedroom, there was only one thing left out on it: a three hundred page manuscript I'd printed out for revisions, because I didn't have anywhere else to put it.

Two days later, it had sixty thousand other things hanging around it—a comb someone used to brush a strand of hair (because clearly it wasn't their whole head), some toenail clippers that, judging by the residue in it, had been recently used on someone's dirt-encrusted nails, the last year's electric bills, a random wrapper for a cough drop I'm pretty sure I didn't eat, and something unidentifiable—a toenail, perhaps?

You can't leave a single thing out, if you're really interested in achieving a tidy home. The law of entropy (otherwise known as "If you leave a shirt here, it will turn into a whole pile of shirts, and, probably, boys' dirty underwear, because clearly this pile is the new dirty clothes hamper, even though no one in the house actually knows how it all got there, because, again, the law of entropy) will win. Every time.

Any job worth doing is worth finishing, is what I always say. I don't always walk the walk, but I'm really good at talking the talk.

The problem is, when it come to finishing, I'd really rather lie in my bed and read, because it's been an overwhelming evening, and the boys are still getting out of their beds claiming they have to go potty, even though when I check on them ten minutes later, they're dancing with the plunger.

So, I don't know, maybe I shouldn't even try. If I can't do it right, why should I do it at all? I'm just making more work for myself. (Husband would interject here that I'm a delightfully positive person to know. I'm relatively sure he's just joking, because I'm actually a pretty big pessimist, which is why me and the law of entropy get along well together, because I can point to that thing Husband put on the banister to "put away later" and let him know that "Entropy is coming to get that," and he'll just look at me like I'm crazy, because of course he knows I'm right, but he doesn't want to admit it. Who's laughing three days later when that one coffee cup has turned into three forks, two bowls, five more coffee cups, twelve plates, and fifteen spoons? Not me. But still. I win. But not really.)

Here are some of the places entropy most likes to play:

1. The sink.

My dishes multiply like rabbits, and it's not because there are eight of us. I'll load the dishwasher, with nothing left in the sink but a single fork that didn't make it in before I pressed start, and when I come down from my work shift, there are now at least fourteen cups that need to be loaded—and there were only six people hanging out downstairs who know how to drink out of a cup. Explain that math to me, please.

2. Our bed.

I used to have this habit of making my bed and then piling all the things that were on the floor on top of the bed, with the intention of putting them away at some point during the day. You know, chipping away at the mess as I had the time. And then a boy would get his foot stuck in the crib, even though he wasn't supposed to even *be* in the crib, because he's 3, and another boy would fall off the trampoline because he didn't think about what might happen if he tried to fly to the ground, and a third boy would try to "skate" on two scooters and run into a brick wall. So I gave up on the whole "chipping away at the mess on my bed."

The bed used to attract a lot of junk. But now the floor does.

3. The coffee table.

I've never seen so many papers. But you can bet there will be more tomorrow.

4. The basket in our kitchen.

It's supposed to be reserved only for important school papers, but if I leave school papers in the basket, they will attract a billion other school papers that should really be in the recycling, because they're worksheets I'd never keep. At least five worksheets come home with each boy every day, and there's no possible way to keep all of that. I'd be crazy to try.

Halfway through the week, I get a little burned out on sorting through all the papers, so this basket quickly overflows, spilling onto the counter, which spills onto the floor, which spills out the doors, and pretty soon we're practically swimming in papers.

I give up.

5. The carpet.

We have a crawling baby now, which means everything he finds on the floor goes right into his mouth. We vacuum all the time, but I swear if there's one other thing that is left on the floor, all the other things on the bottom of my boys' feet or in their hands or hidden inside their pockets will find that one other thing. So baby boy has quite a pile of Things That Go In His Mouth, and I feel pretty much powerless to stop it.

I dig it out of his mouth, he puts something back in. I dig it out, he puts something else in. I dig that out, he's ready with something else. It's the best game ever.

6. My 3-year-olds' faces.

They never wipe their faces. They're old enough to, and we've taught them to wash their hands and faces before and after meals, but do they? Well, that's questionable. Whatever they have on their face is sticky, so, of course, all the other things find a way to that stickiness and stay there. There is dirt, there is snot, and there is wind. Yes, wind. Because in Texas, when the wind is blowing, you can sometimes see it, because it's blowing dust and cedar and all the other things you don't really want to be breathing. It all ends up on my twins' faces.

Their faces also attract berry smoothie, peanut butter they got into when I wasn't manning the place as well as I should have, the juice from black beans, pollen from the flowers they rub all over their cheeks, grass they like to eat, dirt they like to eat, bugs they like to eat. (Notice a pattern here? They've never been sick. It's quite disgustingly amazing.)

7. My 6-year-old's pants.

I don't know what's with these pants. Maybe my 6-year-old uses them as a napkin. Or maybe they never get washed. For some reason, he has this pair of pants, bright green, that are perpetually dirty. It doesn't matter how many times I wash them. (I remember them going through the last clothes cycle, because I poured dish soap all over them, which is my best attempt at stain remover.) As soon as he puts them on, there's a new stain coming at him. Pretty sure those won't make it through the other four. We'll just cut it off here.

8. The boys' bathroom counters.

Every so often, Husband and I will elect not to lock our twins in their bedroom. What always (without fail) happens is one of them (still haven't figured out who) will wander. He will sneak into his bathroom, open a cabinet he's been told again and again not to even touch, take out his toothpaste and paint the counter with it. You don't know sticky until you've tripped over some sweat pants the boys left on their bathroom floor and planted your hand on a toothpaste-painted counter to catch yourself. I peeled half my skin off trying to get out of that trap.

This delightful ritual (paint, clean it up, paint, clean it up) has so far attracted two flies and a handful of gnats. Because bathrooms are gross. Especially the ones belonging to boys.

Entropy is a force to be dealt with, but it will never be mastered. So if you're not going to do it right, I say don't do it at all.

Now I'll just go recline on the couch while my kids tear my house apart. There's not enough time to clean it all up, so why try?

The Tidying Effort Transforms Your Life (Tidying Myths Debunked)

Your Possessions Don't Want to Help You; They Want to Make You Crazy

The hardcore tidying experts are great at spouting mystical things, like how we should greet our house and thank it. Sometimes I can get on the bandwagon. Sometimes not so much.

Recently, I stumbled upon this one: Your possessions want to help you.

False.

See, I can totally understand that being the case when you don't have kids, but when you do have kids, all their possessions are trying to do is help them, which means they're working against you, because kids are always working against parents in the tidying battle. And so that means, if I'm using the philosophy skills I learned in college, our kids' possessions (which are, arguably, really *our* possessions, since we most likely bought them) are not, in fact, trying to help us (especially that noisy truck that sings a ridiculously annoying song, even though it has no batteries).

It doesn't help me, crayons, to necessitate the redoing of tidying my house every single day because one boy decided he wanted to dump you out so he could find that particular shade of orange called "macaroni and cheese" and then he's "too tired" to clean you up. Clean up yourself, crayons. (How many times have I wished it were possible?)

It's also doesn't help me, Discarded Toy, to reappear after I've already bagged you up and set you out in the pick-up trash bin a billion times. When you keep coming back, I keep having to hide you from my kids so they forget they ever had you in the first place, because if they remember they had you in the first place, they'll convince themselves that you are just the most wonderful toy in the whole wide world and that they'll play with you every single day for the rest of their lives if I'll only let them keep you, and that's just not right. It's just not right. I've already done the work. I've cleaned out all the toys my kids haven't played with since they were 2, and I'm sorry that you're one of those, but you have got to go. Stay gone, please.

It doesn't help me, LEGOs, when you stay hidden between the fibers of the carpet so I think when I barricade your bins behind the locked door of our garage, I'll be safe when I kneel down on the floor to change the baby's diaper. Surprise, surprise. My knee is promptly mauled by a tiny little headlight from the Star Wars ship my 8-year-old never built because he thought he could make something cooler from the pieces and then he got distracted from that goal and dumped all of you into a general bin where you'll never, ever, ever be separated again (We've tried. It's not worth it. It would take a thousand years to sort through those LEGOs and build the things they were intended to build. Sorry, LEGOs. I really wanted to see you, Star Wars Desert Outpost. Maybe in another life.).

So, no, my possessions most certainly do not want to help me. In fact, I'm pretty sure they've turned against me, because, for some reason, I keep randomly finding my own books on the floor in front of the shelves in my room, as if they are spontaneously launching themselves from their places, just to be noticed. Maybe that means I have too many books. I don't know. I just know that I'm always bending down to get them and putting them back on my shelf, and if there's one thing I really hate doing, it's doing something twice. Which means I've been living a dream as a parent. A dream that's been held up to a funhouse mirror. Re-shelve the same books. Pick up the same stray toys. Pack away the same old stuffed animals.

If my possessions wanted to help me, they would put themselves back away, because they understand how exhausting it is by the time we make it to our last story time of the day, when the boys (it never fails) are asking us to read three books, instead of two, and when they each pick one, fourteen fall off the shelf. All those books are supposed to be re-shelved, but the boys either don't have the fine motor skills yet or their hands are broken, so those books just end up stacked on a chair where no one is able to sit for days on end, because everyone's too lazy to lift a hand around here. (The other day my 8-year-old told me he doesn't like cleaning up messes that aren't his, and, of course, the mess he was being asked to clean wasn't his. I just laughed maniacally in his face, because I'm a fantastic mother.)

So, possessions, just walk back to where you belong. Go on. Do it. You'll be doing me a favor, I promise. Or better yet, walk yourself out to the trash can that's probably still sitting on the curb, because Husband hardly ever gets around to putting it away until we get a letter from our neighborhood association. Open the lid, make yourself comfortable inside. If you do that, I can pretend like I never saw you splayed out on the floor like you own this living room.

That's what it means to help.

Put Your House in Order, Discover the Secrets to Life

Tidying experts claim that if you put your house in order, you will magically discover what you really want to do with your life.

If it sounds too good to be true, it is.

Because children.

Have I mentioned that children make tidying a house completely and thoroughly difficult? Not just difficult but impossible? (I don't usually like to use extremes, but I think we can all agree on this one, can't we?) It's like you're a hopeful protagonist in your own tidy-house story, and your children are the most clever antagonists, working against you at every move of the game, except it's not a game, and it's not funny, and it's definitely not anything close to fun.

Tidying gurus say that all you have to do is pick up all the "stuff" in your house and make sure it has a place, and then you'll have cleared out enough space in your mind, somehow, to figure out what you were born to do.

What if what you really want to do with your life is get your house in order, so what you want to do never, ever happens, because you can never summon enough motivation to even get started, and then your house never cooperates with you, because what house cleans itself (and if there is one, can I please get it)? It's a joke to ask kids to clean, because their idea of putting clothes away is stuffing them into a drawer and then complaining about how they don't have any shirts hanging in their closet and did you even do laundry this week? Ha ha. So funny.

Their idea of tidying is putting things into a neat little pile, which is what they learned from their daddy, and then letting it sit there, collecting dust and paper and stale bread and other things you don't really want to know about, until that pile becomes massive and intimidating and you start to wonder if you're the only one who can see it, because everyone else acts like it's invisible.

A neat little pile doesn't stay neat for long, even with the best of intentions.

Kids' idea of clean and tidy is pushing everything under a bed or in their closets until you walk into their room and take a good whiff and nearly pass out from the noxious fumes—which are about as bad as their farts—and decide you better locate whatever that is before it eats your whole house down. So, if you're me, you'll go searching through all the mess, and you'll finally locate this old snack container that disappeared three months ago, and you don't want to open it, you don't want to open it, you don't want to open it, but when you pick it up, it leaves a little puddle of gross on the carpet, and it's still dripping, IT'S DRIPPING ON YOUR HANDS, so you fling it across the room, because IT'S DRIPPING ON YOUR HANDS, and it hits the door, because you threw it unnecessarily hard, and it splits and flings—what is that? Apple? Grape? Some new species of mold?—against the walls and shoes you just put in your basket.

(The moral of that story: Don't go looking for the source of bad smells. Make your partner do it. Rather, ask really nicely. Bribe, if you have to. Husband sometimes wonders why I make cookies in the middle of the week. It only takes a little bit of imagination to figure that out.)

Fortunately, I already know (mostly) what I want to do, and, for me, the untidy house helps me along that goal, because I just wrote a whole book about the impossibility of tidying up after children.

Unfortunately, no one else can do it now.

The bad news about this impossibility is that we pretty much signed up for it as parents. The good news is, we get multiple opportunities (an hour) to practice overcoming our own neuroses.

But what I'm really trying to say is that we better start out our parenting journey knowing already what it is we want to do. Because if the only way to figure it out is a tidy house, then we're up a creek full of dirty diapers.

(Personally, I believe there are other ways of discovering what it is you want to do, and they have nothing to do with a perfectly tidy house. So don't lose heart.)

Otherwise, we'll just have to resign ourselves to "wanting" to be a parent for the rest of our lives.

Which actually doesn't sound all that bad, does it?

I mean, we already have the evidence of kids living inside our house. We only have to look at the smudged mirrors and the crayon-colored walls and the buckets of food they drop under the table every meal. They all tell the story of who we are.

There are more important things to worry about than making sure our house is tidy so we can discover what we want to do with our lives. Like making sure the 3-year-old twin isn't getting that toy we just threw away back out of the trash because we specifically remember it being in the direct path of our 6-year-old's puke when he let loose yesterday, and we really, really don't want to clean out all those gears and pockets. Or making sure the other 3-year-old isn't getting into the honey, because for some reason he likes opening it and pouring it into his mouth and eating it raw and thick, which is close to the most annoying thing we've ever seen, because most of the time, the stream of honey doesn't even make it into his mouth but winds up all over the floor. Or the 5-year-old sticking his finger into the butter and eating a whole stick while our backs are turned trying to wrestle the honey from a 3-year-old's vice grip. Or the 8-year-old getting more papers out because he really wants to draw, but it's actually time for bed. Or the 6-year-old changing clothes, again, because he got a single drop of water on the shirt he was wearing and he doesn't like to be wet.

Much more important things. Who needs figuring out what you want to do with your life when you're just trying to survive?

Tidying Language is Lost in Translation

There is something every parent should know before they attempt this climbing-Mt-Everest-without-an-oxygen-pack-or-a-partner-or-warm-clothes task of tidying up a house: Children will follow along behind you and undo all your hard work.

There are a few times a year when I decide I've had enough of my filthy house. Most of these times are not weekends we've sent kids away with their grandparents and could actually tackle tidying and cleaning without kids underfoot, because who wants to spend a weekend without kids cleaning? Nope.

So most of the time, when I'm fed up with filthy, my kids are home, waiting to undo everything.

If both parents try to tackle the project, it's much worse. One day Husband went upstairs to clean, while I was downstairs trying to clean, and no one was really paying attention to the 3-year-old twins, and they unraveled three rolls of toilet paper and tried to see how much of it they could stuff in the toilet with the plunger. I was in the kitchen, trying to scrub the counters that hadn't been wiped down in too long by anyone other than an in-a-hurry-to-get-my-chore-done boy.

Once I turned on the vacuum cleaner, the boys saw it as their free pass to take out All the Stuff because Mama couldn't hear them.

Every now and then—not often—I get a REALLY wild hair and decide I have to clean everything—under couches, under the stove, under the refrigerator, the tops of everything you can't really see and usually leave to the dust. I'll move all the furniture and find stockpiles of Hot Wheels and broken pencils and crayons and food they're not even supposed to eat in the living room. The problem is, as soon as I pull any of it out, the boys take off with it. They'll play with the cars, they'll sharpen the pencils, they'll eat month-old bread (I know. Gross). I don't even have a chance to put it all in the trash before it's already disappeared.

I guess, in reality, that saves me a step—putting it all away—but they really only end up displacing it somewhere else in the house, where it will most likely find its way back underneath the couch.

On these not-so-frequent, clean-everything days, I'll tell them, "We're cleaning the house today" but to them, these words have no meaning. That's not true. They have meaning. It's just a different translation.

Children don't understand cleaning and tidying language.

"We're cleaning the house today" means get out all the papers and scribble one little thing on them and call it finished, and then, when you're tired of that, take out a few books to read and make sure you leave them on the floor, and then, when you're tired of that, go outside and play for three seconds and bring in forty rocks for Mama—make sure you say they're for Mama, because this is how you know they'll definitely be kept, except this time Mama is being really mean, and she makes you take them back outside, and she's the worst mother ever. Well, fine, you just won't give her anything anymore, then. At least until you see those weeds in the yard with the purple flowers and pick them all so you can toss the bouquet at Mama, because she's vacuuming, and it's the perfect time to throw pretty things at her.

"No more toys out right now," means, sure, Mama is cleaning, trying to pick up all the stray cars, and you're not supposed to play with any toys right now, but there's still the art cabinet, she didn't say the art cabinet was off limits, so you go and take all the little cups with the crayons out, even though you only really need one, oh, and make sure you open the bottom cabinet and take out fifteen of the coloring books, even though it's not even possible to color in that many at a time. Be sure to make the rest of them topple over so they fall completely out of the cabinet. Color for a few seconds, and then forget that's what you wanted to do. Go upstairs to your room and find the hundred things you're going to bring back down with you and then, when you're bored with making that kind of mess, go into the pantry, because Mama's not looking, and grab a mason jar of almonds and fill it with roly polies, after you eat all the almonds, of course, and then bring them back in and hide them in the pantry so Mama will never know you ate a half pound of almonds in one day.

"The bathroom is off-limits for the next thirty minutes" means Mama will be so focused on getting the urine—from toilet misses, not purposeful peeing on the floor—that you'll be able to get into the games cabinet and take out Lord of the Rings Risk, with its billions of tiny little pieces, which you know she must hate, since she's always telling Daddy they should get rid of it, and he's always saying he can't get rid of it, because when you're older you'll want to play it with him, and you think, of course, that it's the best game ever, because A BILLION PIECES (!) you can spread all over the floor Mama just vacuumed. Make sure you dump them ALL out and, when you've put them all on the Middle Earth map, decide it's probably time for a break, and leave the pieces where they are so your 3-year-old brothers can knock them all off and they'll slide under the couches and make Mama mad—but you're off the hook, because the twins did it.

"I'll only be upstairs for a minute" means you now have the opportunity to follow along behind Mama as she picks up every single stray book on the library floor and shelves it, biding your time until she moves into your bedroom to make sure it's clean, and then your little brothers' bedroom to make sure they didn't empty the closets again. Wait until she's in her bedroom, because she always gets stuck in there, and then pull down all those titles in the Harry Potter series, because before you start to read one of them, you must, naturally, see them all. Leave them on the floor, because book carpets are the best.

"Everybody stay out of the dining room" means that while Mama's wiping down the table and cleaning all the glass, it's your job to sneak all those cups down from the cabinet and fill them with water and put three of the Lord of the Rings Risk pieces in them and then into the freezer to see what happens to figurines when they freeze. Mama will probably never notice. Grin to yourself, because you've just successfully thwarted all your parents' efforts to clean and tidy the house.

One Trick to Tidying: Don't Get Attached to the Past

I have something that still hangs in my closet, no matter how many times I've tried to clean it out.

That thing is my wedding dress.

It's still in the original protective bag, not even preserved or anything, and those white gloves I used to wipe my nose while I was crying so hard during the ceremony (and, grossly, used to hold my beloved's hands again—a test in what he was willing to endure), are in a clear little ziplock bag hanging off the back. Neither the dress nor the gloves have ever been washed. I know. So sanitary.

I'm relatively sure that I wouldn't be able to fit into this dress again right now, because I've had six children and I was slim and svelte when I first got married. But still it hangs in my closet. For what? I don't really know. I mean, I do have dreams of one day wearing it for Halloween, painting my face as a zombie bride, hanging on the arm of Husband, who will don a tux he had from high school that he used for choir concerts (which also doesn't fit him anymore, strangely). We would be the hit of the block, with little zombie children trailing the streets behind us.

It's not easy to get rid of things that have such a strong tie to the past. When I take out that wedding dress, which is about once every few years, I remember the day I said, "I do," how it was raining and how I cried, because I'd planned an outdoor wedding, and we had to move the location at the last minute, because I held out hope all day, but, sadly, hope doesn't prevent rain. I remember the smells of that old musty church that had been around longer than my great-grandmother, sitting in a wheelchair up front. I remember the look on Husband's face.

Or maybe I just have evidence of it all in pictures.

Tidying experts say there are two reasons people keep things instead of just tossing them. One of those reason is attachment to the past. Another is anxiety about the future.

I have a hard time with the first, but I have an even harder time with the second.

You see, I'm a cheapskate. If I think something can be reused and save us a buck or two, I'm going to keep it. That's why we have bins and bins of threadbare clothes in our garage, because there's still one more boy to wear them, and I am not going to buy new clothes for the last baby in our house. So we just keep all the old clothes and he has a ready-made wardrobe. Sure, they have a few stains, and all the knees on the pants are blown out, but ragged is cool, right?

Husband was raised in much the same way I was: by frugal parents who didn't really have the disposable income to be ostentatious or extravagant. And so, together, we make quite the case for keeping something even though we'll probably never need it again.

In our garage is a large bin of cords. I have no idea which electronic devices lent their cords to this collection. The technology expert in our house, the 3-year-old, doesn't either. And, surprise, neither does Husband. He does wonder, in just the right amount, if he might need all those cords someday, so into a bin the cords go.

Last time he searched the bin for an hour to find a match to the boys' CD players, but none of the three thousand cords fit. Go figure.

These are the kinds of crazy things you keep when you're raised frugal.

There's this fear that accompanies throwing things away, because you're afraid you might someday need them. I feel it every time I'm cleaning out my closet and I come across a pair of jeans that are in perfect condition, except that they're from high school, and the body that wore them was 17 years old instead of thirty. Yet I hang onto them because they're in perfect condition, and you never know—someday I might be able to squeeze into them. I just have to stay away from Trader Joe's toffee. Which is so easy—but I'll start tomorrow.

I feel the fear when I see those shirts I wore in college—especially the one that had one shoulder exposed and was skin tight, because what if there's an occasion to wear that again—except that if there were, I wouldn't want to wear it, because my shoulders have grown right along with the rest of me.

I feel the fear when I open that closet full of old blankets, because what if one of the boys' blankets wears out? We'll need to have these other blankets at the ready, because we bought them, and they're not worn out, and, besides, who gets rid of blankets? You can always use blankets.

It's a crazy way to live.

I'm not a hoarder, by any means, but if anything has any kind of purpose in the future, I have a very difficult time getting rid of it.

Over the years, my boys got really good at this stage we'll call "Tearing All the Papers Out of a Book." We would try to give them a book to read in their beds during nap time, and then we would come back into their bedroom five minutes later, and all the pages had been ripped from the binding. And so we would tell them they couldn't have books for a while, and then a month later we'd try again, and it was the same old story. So now I have a laundry basket in my closet full of old book pages that would be great for crafts. Except I never get around to those crafts because kids. Six of them. And even though the closet is just about bursting with all these "future" craft projects, I keep adding more, because I can totally see the finished product in my head, and it's amazing. I don't want to give all this away. I want to use it for myself.

I did try to do one of these projects recently. I brought out all the torn pages from one of our favorite books, *The Great Paper Caper*, by Oliver Jeffers, and I decorated a box to be used in our home library as a "books to re-shelf" stacking place. The whole time we worked on the project, the boys were exclaiming their pleasure, saying things like, "This is so boring," "Why do we have to do this?" and, my favorite, "Why do I have to spend time with my family and work on this stupid art project?"

They thoroughly enjoyed themselves, which, of course, made me want to do more projects like that. (Future projects planned: Covering Up the Drawings on the Couch. Sanding Down the Piano Bench that Shoots Splinters Into our Backside. And, also, A Picture of Mama When She Was Skinny.)

The question that shakes its finger in my face every time I think about whether or not I should throw something away is: But what if I need it someday?

Someday works against our aspirations to keep a tidy house.

Especially when kids are so great at digging through bins with junk saved for someday and deciding that someday is today. They'll make a creature out of all those old cords. They'll play dress-up with an off-the-shoulder shirt. They'll "sort through" all the ripped pages of the books you've collected over the years and then they'll forget to put them back.

Just do yourself a favor. Get rid of it.

But I'll keep the jeans. I'm sure I'll be able to fit a leg inside them someday.

How Can You Be Surrounded by Joy in a Wrecked House?

Another common mantra in the tidying world is that when you're surrounded by what sparks joy, you will become joyful.

Well, I'm surrounded by children, and most minutes, when they're not sparking irritation, they are bringing great joy.

They are, of course, one of the most joyful pieces of my life. Also one of the hardest. But one of the best. They are the ones who take me to the highest highs and drag me to the lowest lows, and they are the ones who show me sorrow that can then be measured against my joys. They are the ones who smile at me in that particular way that makes all my limbs start to melt, because I see a flash of the little boy he used to be, the one who would climb into my lap and actually stay. They are the ones who disarm me with one "I love you so much," and they are the ones who bind me with their kisses, and they are the ones who show me how sacrificial love can be, because, when they bring me a flower and call me the most beautiful girl in the world, I'll do anything for them—even pick up dirty, smelly soccer socks, turn them right side out, and put them in the laundry basket that he probably didn't even notice was here, because he was so intent on making it to his room so he could finish that striped, use-all-the-colors-in-the-crayon-box heart he later cut out and left on my bedside table with a "For you, Mama, with all my love" note. Even dig the poop out of their nails when they decide that playing with feces looks like fun. Even clean up the vomit that sprayed all over my bed and face when they felt sick and needed to come tell me about it.

They are the ones who leave little maddening papers around the house that I'll pick up and, every now and then, find a precious treasure hidden within—a story about how much they love their brothers and their mama and daddy and how they don't really want to grow up, because they have the best life now. They are the ones who write little love notes on furniture, even though they know they're not supposed to, and they are the ones who pick the roses in the front yard that they've been told not to pick, because they wanted something beautiful for Mama, and they are the ones who weave words around our table that are more imaginative, more innocent, more profound than any award-winning novel.

It's not the *things* around us that bring the most joy. It's not the thousands of books that contain thousands of stories and vital information, no matter how much we enjoy reading. It's not the musical instruments we still tinker with on occasion, even though we gave up the band for kids. It's not the shoes or the jeans that fit or the writing notebooks or the memorabilia or the pictures or the art supplies or the toys or the televisions or the treadmill we use once a year or the bed where we get to sleep when we've wrestled them all down for the night.

It's the people. The people are what make life worth living, and I get to have seven of them surrounding me at every moment. And even though they often seem like an entirely different species, they are living in my house every day, every night, which means that I'm constantly, every moment—even when I'm in the bathroom and they're too old to be here listening to me empty my bladder—surrounded by joy. Also madness, but mostly joy. And this makes joy, at least some of the time, quite easy to find.

It's true that sometimes being surrounded doesn't always seem like something that sparks joy, because there are six little people incessantly talking and asking for things, and they don't always use their perfect manners. And the craziness of a day can bury joy like a day-old corpse, because I just looked in the cabinet, and there are not enough dishes to even set the table for dinner tonight, since someone forgot to press start on the dishwasher last night. Sometimes there's a running commentary taking place in my head that sounds a little like, *I can't do this anymore, I'm not equipped to handle all of this, I don't know what to do, I don't know if I'm doing this right, I don't know how to keep on keeping on, I need help and there's no help, why can't they just leave me alone, will I ever know what it's like to have alone time again, why are they so obsessed with figuring out where my pee comes from, can you just let me get dressed in peace, please take your hands off me, get up off the floor or I might end up down there with you, please stop screaming because it's making me want to scream and I really don't want to scream, why is this happening, why them, why me,* and all of that can steal joy if we're not diligent about holding tight to it.

But when I think about the way that I clean out a room, going through all the different corners, picking up all the objects, examining it, determining whether I really need or want it or can I find a place for it, I wonder if I can examine my children with the same diligence. Of course I need them. Of course I want them. Of course they have a place, because they are my child.

I examine them, and I see the way that smile lights up his eyes, and I see the way love walks him back out of anger, and I see their hopes and dreams and plans all contained in an amazing kid-body, and I marvel that I get to be the keeper of such great joy.

It doesn't happen every moment, of course. But if I'm looking for it, if I don't forget to find the joy in the moment, I see it. I am surrounded by joy because I am surrounded by my children. It's true that sometimes that joy is grudging, because I just had to pick up six thousand stickers off the carpet and the cabinet and the dining room table (why do coloring books come with stickers now? I was just fine with coloring books when I was a kid, manufacturers. Because the point is to color. STOP GIVING US STICKERS!). But sometimes all it takes is one look, and, bam, it hits me right in the chest, that single, overarching thought.

What was I thinking?

I mean, I am surrounded by the brightest joy that ever lived.

Tidying Increases Good Fortune

Tidying experts also claim that tidying increases good fortune.

No wonder I have such bad luck as a parent. Just this morning I was walking down the stairs, and I tripped over something that Husband had stacked there, because his idea of tidying is stacking stuff on the stairs. I broke my foot a few months ago for this very reason and we all talked about how everyone in the house should work hard to leave the stairs clear because Mama trips over her own feet and doesn't need any help in the I-almost-died department.

That time, I tripped at the bottom of the stairs and broke my foot. This time I was teetering at the top. Fortunately, I was able to catch myself using the banister (it's a little loose now), which I hugged all the way down, and I guess that could be considered good fortune, because I didn't break my neck today.

Last week I was winning at parenting, and I got my boys off to school on time and walked them all the way and kissed them at the door, and then we made it back to the house and I had some time before the twins usually start terrorizing everything and everyone, so I got dinner started in a crockpot. Except when I dropped the ceramic bowl in the crockpot, I didn't know I'd already turned it on, and so when I touched the metal heater, it shot its unmerciful fire all the way into the side of my hand. But I guess that was actually good fortune, because at least I turned it on this time, and we didn't get to dinnertime only to have raw chicken sitting in its own blood, while six boys complained that they were starving. Also, it had to be good fortune that I only burned the side of my hand and not my entire hand, because I needed that hand to grab the butcher knife my 3-year-old took out of the dishwasher while I was moaning about my burn. See? He didn't kill anyone today. Good fortune.

The other day I had just reorganized the art cabinet, where we keep papers and art supplies so the boys have easy access to it, and when I turned my back because the timer on the dryer had just gone off and I needed to get one load out and put another in, the twins, who are the greatest opportunists in the whole world, decided they were going to take the stubs of color pastels, which they're forbidden to use, which means color pastels are delightfully enticing, and draw all over their car track and the stairs and the floor right in front of the dining room table, so by the time I closed the dryer door, made sure the dryer started (because one dryer-didn't-start load means I'll be doing laundry all day tomorrow, too) and walked back out, I met a masterpiece of red twirls extending all behind the couch and hand-drawn spiders walking all the way up the stairs. When I asked them if they had done it, they said, no, their brother who was at school had done it, and I remained calm and collected and informed them there would be no more coloring today and they could either go outside to play or sit in their booster seats, where I could watch them, until lunchtime—and I suppose this was good fortune, because I didn't give one of them away today.

And then there was the night I was making pancakes without really paying attention, because someone had just dumped out their glass of milk, and someone else (me) had to clean it up, because 3-year-olds are quite incompetent at mopping milk, it turns out, and the only reason I turned back to the stove was because the smoke alarms started shrieking. And I guess this, too, is good fortune, because the house didn't burn down, and, also, I got to teach the kids how to crawl on the floor in case of a fire, so they don't end up with smoke inhalation damage to their lungs. We all crawled to the front and back doors so we could open them and release ourselves from the heavy cloud hanging over our heads. So, yeah. Fortunate.

Now that I think of it like this, I really do have more good fortune than bad fortune. It's all in the way you look at things, I guess. All the bad fortune has a little bit of good fortune, because it could always be worse, right?

I'm sorry, tidying experts, but I have a really hard time believing that my good fortune is related to the state of my house, because 6.9 out of 7 days, my house is a national-disaster wreck. And good fortune and bad fortune seem to come in equal measure.

Unless I haven't actually experienced genuine good fortune because my house hasn't been perfectly tidy since the beginning of parenthood. Maybe, if it were, I'd actually be losing weight instead of gaining another pound or five every year. Maybe my kids would look at me and think, "She's cool. I'm so glad she's my mom." Maybe we'd win the lottery without even buying a ticket.

Maybe the house would clean itself or kids would suddenly take an interest in tidying up or, better yet, I'd become Mary Poppins. I've always wanted to be Mary Poppins.

Make me Mary Poppins, house.

Then I'd be a believer.

Oh, wait. I'd actually have to put in some effort and tidy. Never mind. I'll just be content with trying to see my bad fortune as good fortune and save myself the energy expenditure. I'm sure I'll need it. Tonight's homemade pizza night, and the twins woke up with I'll-get-into-the-plunger-and-show-Mama-how-good-I-am-at-plunging-the-toilet-with-diarrhea-in-it-if-it's-the-last-thing-I-do on their mind.

The Confidence You Gain in Your Tidying Attempts: You Will Fail at Lesser Things

Tidying experts say that, among many other amazing things, you can gain confidence from the tidying up of your home. I agree. But I think we may be talking about two different things, because the confidence I believe can be gained from trying to tidy your house when children live in it is this:

You will fail at lesser things.

You will fail, one day, at beating your 8-year-old son at chess, because he's in a club and you were never all that great at it, anyway, even though you tell yourself you used to be super smart. It was probably all a ruse.

You will fail at a cutting your boys' hair the one time you try, because you were too cheap to pay the nominal fee you'd pay for a little boy's haircut, and they'll end up looking like a bowl sat on their heads while you chopped away.

You will fail at finding your keys when the kids have just used them to unlock the playroom, which is not really a playroom anymore but has become an obstacle course, a massive junk drawer, a "Hazard—Keep Out" kind of place. It didn't used to be, but then you canceled your storage space, with the intention of cleaning out everything in it. Everything in it ended up in your garage, or playroom. But back to the keys. When your kids used them, they fell somewhere in this obstacle course of a room. Too bad you don't have a location device on them. You're probably never going to leave the house again.

You will fail at keeping up with school papers.

You will fail at remaining cool as your kid begins to care about cool. It doesn't matter how many books you write or how many full-length albums you produce or how many beautiful art pieces you paint in the clip of a year. You are totally uncool, Mom and Dad.

You will fail at finishing those cloth napkins you planned to make for them when they all went off to kindergarten. And, at the same time, you will fail at finishing the crocheted blanket you were supposed to make for his sixth birthday and the other one you were supposed to make for the baby on his first birthday, because there's just no time left. All your time is spent hanging out with the kids. That's what you'll tell yourself. It's really spent signing school folders.

You will fail at kicking a ball past the little boy who now runs faster than you do, mostly because you have two 3-year-old cling-ons hanging to your leg, because this is how they said it would be a fair game of kickball.

You will fail at trying to learn how to roller blade when you turn 30.

You will fail at finishing that book in the time you thought you'd finish it, because boys make it nearly impossible to read.

You will fail at making your bed every morning.

You will fail at cooking a breakfast of fried eggs and pancakes, because there's just not enough time, and, besides, they don't want to wait that long.

You will fail at remembering whether the dishwasher was already run.

You will fail at hanging up laundry the day you wash it.

You will fail at shelving books every night, because by the time all the kids are down in bed, you have just enough energy to crawl to your bed and lie down.

You will fail at keeping your bedroom door closed any night, because at least one of the children will come knocking with something of emergency proportions, even if it's just to tell you what their fart smelled like. Or that they love you. Both equally important.

You will fail at keeping even one puzzle with all the puzzle pieces.

You will fail at making sure the game of Operation doesn't have any pieces missing.

You will fail at finding a full and complete deck of cards anywhere in your house.

You will fail at keeping toothpaste off the counters of their bathroom.

You will fail at keeping a toilet to yourself, because there's always a time when they're talking to you and they have to go right this minute, even though their toilet is only fifteen steps away.

You will fail at recycling those boxes before your kids see them and decide they want to make new toys out of them, and most of the time you'll be glad that they're so creative.

You will fail at keeping your plants alive and healthy.

You will fail at remembering to water your plants (sorry plants).

You will fail at cooking a perfect grilled cheese sandwich, because when your back was turned, your ears picked up on some suspicious splashing in the bathroom, and you know that sound, you know it well, so you investigated, and, sure enough, it was your 3-

year-old, trying to plunge the toilet, even though he's been told a billion times to keep his hands off.

You will fail at remembering that things you said you could never forget. (What was it again? You have no idea.)

You will fail at trying not to make the sex talk with your kids awkward. It will always be awkward. Embrace awkward.

You will fail at keeping up with the lawn outside, because boys are constantly digging holes, and who has the time to cut grass when you're just trying to reduce the mayhem that crops up in your house?

You will fail at trying to stay the same. Because when you're a parent, your kids are constantly, day by day, hour by hour, shaping who you become—and who you become is better.

So, really, what failing at keeping a tidy house really affords you is the confidence that you will fail at many, many other things, and that you will be better, greater, stronger for your failing.

Bring it on.

The Real Story of Tidying Up (Or What Kids Do to a Home)

All the Shoes that Never Make it to the Shoe Basket

Several years ago, Husband and I designated a basket beside the front door as the Shoe Basket. So when kids came home from anywhere and wanted to take off their shoes, (because kids still prefer bare feet when it's 150 degrees out even though the backyard is full of only brambles since all the grass has fried), they would have a place to put them.

Kids will go barefoot anywhere. Once I had to carry my infant son on one arm and my 6-year-old on the other, because he thought he had some shoes in the car—not where they belong! We have a basket for that!—and it turns out those shoes actually were *not* in the car where he thought he'd left them, and we were already late for the doctor's appointment by the time we arrived, which is when he bothered to tell me he had no shoes, so we couldn't very well turn back around and go home. I suspect he just wanted to go to the doctor's appointment without shoes.

What he received for his troubles was a long lecture on the importance of making sure his shoes got where they go. That lecture, of course, went in one ear and out the other. He retained all of zero words. That's an educated guess, by the way, compiled using the number of times his shoes actually made it to the Shoe Basket after that, which was and still is zero.

It's like feast or famine with our trusty old Shoe Basket. Either we have thirty pairs of shoes waiting for the eight people who live in our house, or we have zero. There are shoes, of course, just no matching pairs. There are fifteen size 3 left shoes. Or seven right foot flip flops that the 5-year-old will have to make work on his left foot, because we're out of time. Or there are one of every size, and the 6-year-old has to wear his older brother's left tennis shoe that's a whole size and a half too large, but at least it matches!

We're a mess when it comes to shoes.

When we actually have time to search for all those mysteriously missing shoes, we'll find them scattered all over the house, one of a pair sitting in the downstairs bathroom trash can along with the soggy toilet paper roll one of the 3-year-olds stuck in the toilet and tried to make go down the "hole" with the plunger, and the other hiding under the couch, two hundred feet away. We will find shoes in the refrigerator and on the bottom shelf of the pantry and closed up with the coloring books in the art cabinet.

At first I didn't understand this. How in the world were shoes getting into these random places? And then I caught the 3-year-old twins playing with their Hot Wheels, stuffing them into shoes and making them fly on a shoe airplane. And while that's really creative play, I also couldn't help thinking about how most of the people in my house claim they can't find socks, because they lose them five hours after I buy them, so they're typically wearing those laced-up kickers without any socks. So there's some stank involved. Trust me, you do NOT want to sniff while you're tying my boys' shoes.

Unfortunately, it's not just the kids who treat our Shoe Basket like it's a suggestion box. It's also Husband. He will take off his shoes while he's sitting watching a movie with the boys on the couch, and he will leave them there so I will trip over them when I'm doing

Burpees the next morning. He will take them off in our bedroom, right beside where I'll lie on the floor to do my ab exercises, and the whole time I'm huffing and puffing I'm wondering where in the world that awful smell, something akin to rotten corn chips mixed with a busted sewage line, is coming from and then, when I'm finally finished and my stomach is on fire along with my nose, I'll crawl to my feet and spot the culprit: His old TOMs that have never seen the luxury of socks between skin and shoe.

After which I'll gently remind him that we not only have a closet where all our shoes can be stored, but we also have a Shoe Basket where he can put them when he's finished wearing them. He'll smile sheepishly and return them where they go, and then the next day I'll trip over another pair on my way to the bathroom.

To tell the truth, I've been occasionally known to leave my running shoes right by the end of my bed, which is definitely not where they go, because I think it makes me more prone to getting up at 5 a.m. and heading out for a run while I have the chance and boys are sleeping. It doesn't. And I shouldn't. But I'm so busy putting away everyone else's shoes I don't have energy left for my own.

So, I surrender. Sorry, Shoe Basket. You deserve to see action, but I suspect it's going to be a very long time before you do.

LEGOs: The Safest Explosion You'll Ever Survive (And Also the Most Annoying)

Let's just talk for a minute about LEGOs.

I love LEGOs. I really do. They are so much fun to play with. I'm just as guilty of spending an afternoon trying to put together a fire station that Spider-Man is trying to save from the bad guys as my kids are.

The problem is that back when we made the decision to start collecting LEGOs, the oldest was already 7, and he really wanted to collect ALL the Star Wars sets. Which was fine, because Husband likes Star Wars, too, and I don't mind it so much either, because George Lucas is about the coolest person in the world. But what we didn't think about when we made the leap was how all of those sets would become one big set.

The oldest has seven different LEGO Star Wars sets, and they somehow became four bins of LEGOs. It would take years to put those sets together the way they were intended to be put together, and I guess I should be thankful for all the things he does with them instead (he made a near exact replica of our house once out of the LEGOs), but the thing is, I really wanted to see what those sets looked like put together, and I never got to. I probably care way more about this than my kid does.

The other, bigger problem is that when it's time to clean up LEGOs, it's pretty much impossible to clean them all up. When we tell our boys it's time to clean up, they'll look at just the one bin they've dumped out and they will already feel completely overwhelmed and unable to complete such a daunting task, because there are a billion tiny little pieces, and even after overcoming that initial resistance and getting started, there's no way they'll put away every piece. Kids are practically blind. It's impossible to clean up all the LEGOs. Some pieces get knocked beneath the carpet in the dining room. Some get shoved under the sofa table behind the couch, and they will surface days after we lock their bins away in the garage, or sometimes they will make an appearance in mere hours, usually because someone has knocked something else out from under the couch and this culprit brings with it an overlooked LEGO piece that either (a) reminds my kids they have LEGOs or (b) remains invisible, trapped in carpet fibers so that the next time I kneel on the floor it will slice my knee cap in half.

When my boys play with LEGOs in our house, the LEGOs can do nothing else but explode. And by explode, I mean they explode—go everywhere imaginable. I've had one in a sock before, and I have no idea how it got there. I've sat on one hiding under the bolted-down cushion of a chair (you think it hurts to step on a LEGO piece? Try sitting on one and you tell me which one hurts more.). I've found them in the boys' shoes, in plant pots, inside the piano bench (someone's trying to play me. There's no way a LEGO piece could crawl into a closed piano bench nook.).

It doesn't matter if there's one bin out or three of them, the mess and its disaster will be exactly the same.

And then, when the 8-year-old decides that he's made the very definition of a masterpiece, he always wants to leave it out, because he does NOT want to break something this amazing, and how do you explain to an 8-year-old that he has 3-year-old brothers who will, at the most inopportune moment, find that masterpiece and not only destroy it but destroy the room in which it sits, fashioning a national disaster that would make a tornado jealous.

LEGOs just aren't a convenient thing to have around in a house full of kids, as much as I love them. They were a good invention. Truly. I understand how they can make kids really good at building the imaginary shapes and buildings and lands that live in their heads, but when it's all said and done, I'm not entirely convinced having them around is worth it. They're like glitter. You try to wipe it away, but it never really goes away, and you'll keep finding glowing specks of it months after you rid yourself and your home of its every trace (or so you think).

I'm not saying we'll get rid of our LEGOs. I'm just saying that somebody, by now, should have invented some sort of LEGO vacuum cleaner that has the power and intelligence to suck up all the LEGO pieces on a floor or between couch cushions or in shoes and empty them out neatly into their designated bin. Although that probably wouldn't be a great idea, because in my home, you'd also be sucking up whole layers of dirt and hair and stale food the kids like to "accidentally" drop when I'm not looking (it all looks suspiciously like spinach). So you'd need two different filters, one for the LEGOs and one for all the other trash, but then what if the vacuum cleaner gets confused and ends up putting the trash in the LEGO bin and the LEGOs in the trash one, and then you just have a bigger mess than when you started. (This is where my mind wanders when my kids are creating worlds with words and all talking at the same time and my brain hits overload.) I'm sure there are much smarter people working on this than me.

We now have the option of renting LEGOs. Which honestly sounds like a nightmare waiting to happen. If we lose library books that are as big as my face, you better believe we're going to lose LEGO pieces.

So I guess we'll just stick with our own. I'm getting callouses from stepping on the invisible ones anyway. Pretty soon LEGO pieces won't be able to penetrate these feet, and I'll give up caring that somebody detonated a bin of LEGOs up in here.

What's That Disgusting Smell? Oh, You Know. Kids.

A house with children will smell like feet and old food and sometimes, if you're really lucky and have a few gassy ones on your hands, sulfur and rotten eggs.

I notice the nasty feet smell every time I bend down to slip on my TOMs so I can walk the boys to school, and it's probably mostly my shoes, but I'm just saying there are also forty other pairs of shoes stacked in that shoe basket when they're not spread randomly all over the house. And I know it's not JUST my shoes that are contributing to the smell that would make a taxidermist pass out. I also notice it when I've gone into their room, which is a repository for dirty socks, apparently. Boys are always complaining that they don't have any clean socks, because they're all sitting in a corner of their room, waiting to be put in the dirty clothes hamper, and I'm not touching them with a fifty-foot high-jump pole.

My boys are notoriously bad at cleaning out their lunch boxes on the weekends. This is mostly because Husband is with them every other afternoon and trains them to put away all their lunch stuff into the sink straightaway. We use reusable containers that need daily washing, and they do it so perfectly for him, and then I get to take over in the afternoons on Fridays, and suddenly they forget everything they're supposed to do. It's like a change of parent means they have no idea what happens next. Aren't we eating breakfast soon? Wait. It's 3:15 p.m.

It doesn't matter how many times I tell them to put all their stuff away, they're already in weekend mode, and they don't think they have to do a single thing related to school.

So, inevitably, what happens is that Monday rolls around and all the lunch containers are missing, and when I go looking, I realize that they're still in their lunch boxes, and there's an awful smell coming from them. Let me just say it doesn't take long for an apple core to go rancid. Or macaroni and cheese. Or the crust of a peanut butter sandwich on homemade wheat bread. I will have the great pleasure of opening these science projects and cleaning them out, gagging and trying not to laugh at how I must sound and appear to anyone who might be watching (no one ever is).

The smell in those containers varies, as does the sight that will joyfully greet me, springing from silver. I've had what looks like it might have been broccoli, except we don't usually send broccoli with the boys, only carrots or cucumbers or corn or edamame, things that are better cold. Maybe it was the vine from red grapes. On second thought, that's probably what it was, but it grew so much green vegetation over the weekend it looked like old broccoli. Shudder.

One thing I can always count on, though, is that there's always a delightful surprise waiting just under the lid. It's like my very own Jack-in-the-Box. You're terrified of that one crank that will make the clown come popping out at you, but you're also just wanting to get it over with. You're controlling the crank, but you're not controlling what's going to jump out at you. It's terrifying.

But the most charming smells in my home are the ones I find in my boys' bathrooms.

Not only are my boys terrible at flushing, no matter how many times they are begged to please get better at this one little thing, they are also really, really bad at aiming. I don't think it's so much that they're bad at aiming as it is that things distract them in the middle of peeing. The other day my 3-year-old twin was standing to pee, and he thought it would be a good idea to stick his finger into the stream, which not only splattered the pee everywhere but also meant that he lost the good grip on his boy-part and sent the urine flying everywhere. And then he tried to overcorrect and shot pee on the back of the toilet, and the room was starting to look like a sprinkler had gone off inside, so I just had to turn away and pretend not to notice. It's not the bathroom I have to use, after all.

When the 8-year-old is using the bathroom, he usually likes to be alone, but no one in our house knows exactly what it means to be alone, because there are so many of us tripping all over each other and it's a smallish house. Inevitably someone will come barging in through the bathroom door, which doesn't have a doorknob right now because we had to use said doorknob on the twins' bedroom door so we could lock them in their room at night. I know how that sounds, but you don't know what fear is until you set two 3-year-olds loose in an everyone-else-is-sleeping house.

After this barging in, the 8-year-old will look up from his impressive state of concentration and yell something at the person who opened the door. He will probably also throw something like a toothbrush to chase the brother out. He wants his privacy, after all. And then he's no better than the 3-year-old at aiming.

I try to ignore this disaster of a bathroom, because it's Husband's and his sons' responsibility to clean it. That actually hasn't happened yet, but when it does, the point is that all that misaimed pee will maybe teach them the importance of Keeping Pee in the Potty.

Somewhere along the way, we became immune to the smell emanating from this sewage facility. One of these days I'll hire a cleaning service to tackle what my stomach cannot handle. For now I just try to enter at my own risk and pretend I don't notice the smell coming from the toilet and the walls. And the floor. And the trash can, which is the last place I'll ever look.

The Whole World's a Canvas (Especially When It Has Walls)

Before we welcomed our first son, we took great time and care to write a Bible verse on the wall of his room, a verse about being strong and courageous and favored, and then we meticulously painted half the wall mustard yellow and the other half a rich blue, because our baby was going to be surrounded by bold colors that would awaken the artist within him.

Or some nonsense like that.

And then, the first time he had quiet time in his room with crayons, those walls we'd worked so hard to paint and decorate were covered with primitive cave drawings.

We patiently painted over his drawings and explained to him that walls were not for drawing pictures on, but he could use paper, and he could have all the paper he wanted, and he said he understood, and he never did it again. And then we had more children, and our hands were so busy trying to keep them all out of the trash and the toilet and the garage where all the junk lives, for now, that occasionally our attention would shift and one kid would break free from parent eyes and before we knew it they'd colored an entire wall red.

And of course we couldn't just forbid them to use crayons, because how would they find their artistic expression if we set them in front of a blank sheet of paper without any drawing supplies and said, "Use your imagination"? But we really didn't want to see all our walls covered in scribbles that could have been a plant or a tiger or something else entirely, like maybe the wind.

It quickly became an impossible thing to regulate, this art and drawing time, because as soon as you took the crayons away from one 3-year-old twin, the other one was having his heyday on the stairs with a slab of red oil pastel, and before you knew it there were curly lines and flourishes leading all the way to your bedroom door, and it would just take too much effort to clean it up. So instead of cleaning up, we gave up.

Of course they know, still, that walls are not for drawing on. But when a new mural shows up, we hardly notice anymore. Eventually, we plan to turn all the walls into hand-painted murals, assigning each boy a wall when they can draw a whale that actually looks like a whale, and we'll take great pride in our artistic walls. For now, we'll just be content with a preview of what's to come: spiders that are supposed to be humans, scribbled all over the twins' closet walls with a crayon they keep hidden God knows where. A red door, courtesy of the 6-year-old when he was 3. A bathroom door with blue pen scribbles that, when you turn your head a certain way, might just look like letters, which the 5-year-old drew when he was 3. (If you haven't noticed, there seems to be a recurring age at which our walls are decorated by budding artists. Seems my kids decide to be wall artists right about the time they turn 3. That's precisely what makes 3-year-olds so delightful, I suppose.)

It doesn't matter who did it, no one will fess up, and most of the time I know exactly who it was, because it's usually the kid who wears the age of 3, as I've already mentioned. My guess is that 3-

year-olds are right in that maddening time when they understand that drawing on the walls isn't allowed but are just young enough to still have zero impulse control when they see a blank spot on the wall that most definitely, no questions asked, no consequences considered, needs to be filled with color. They also seem to think a green scribble would look nice on the floor between the red wine stain my aunt left me one Christmas and the oil spot Husband accidentally made one day when he came in looking like the underside of a car. And they clearly, as if all that isn't enough, think the couch needs some swirly lines, but they'll need a permanent marker for that, thanks for asking.

I thank my lucky stars every time I see a drawing and it's either chalk or crayon, because at least these things are washable if we actually have the energy to pick up a rag, but permanent marker, well, the answer to that is in the name. We try hard to keep permanent markers away from the kids, but somehow they always turn up. They contribute to things like turning a yellow shirt into a black-and-yellow-striped shirt. They make whiskers on cheeks and hair on a forehead, so one of them will go to school looking like a lion, and you'll have to send a note to his teacher. They mark notes on the piano keys, "because it helps me remember which is which," said the one who should have known better.

Kids will always find permanent markers. And I'm telling you, you've never known terror until you notice a permanent marker is missing from the place it was just a few minutes ago. Who has it? What are they doing with it? And worse: What are they planning to do?

We will knock ourselves out trying to find it, and we will not be able to until that next great masterpiece shows up on the bookshelf. How fortunate. There's the marker. Right next to the self portrait that looks like a caterpillar.

Unexpected drawings on all the surfaces of a home—they are the highlight of a parent life. Who else gets to talk about fine art in all the places you would least expect, like the bathroom, when you're sitting on the toilet and notice a new masterpiece on the wall in front of you. Who else gets to call the artist right in and ask them what they were thinking and actually get the answer? Who else gets to call said artist Son or Daughter?

We're surely privileged people.

Where Are All My Household Utensils?

You know what one of my favorite things about living with children is?

Missing things.

The other day I was stirring a pot of mashed potatoes, and I laid down the spatula and went to dig in the freezer for some broccoli I could lay out on a cookie sheet and pour olive oil over and roast in the oven. And then I went to stir the potatoes again, because they were boiling great white foam over the sides of the stainless pot, and my wooden spoon was gone.

None of the boys were around. I hadn't heard anyone come inside or go out. I searched high and low, thinking maybe it had fallen on the floor and I just couldn't see it because I had some unexplainable spoon-shaped blind spot. There aren't many places a bamboo spoon can hide. It wasn't on the floor. I crawled on my hands and knees, just to be sure. So I gave up and took out the metal spoon, which was probably a better one to use anyway. Oh, well. Not a big deal. I probably hadn't stirred them in the first place.

I drained the potatoes and unwrapped the butter to melt in them and shook out some salt and hooked up the mixer so I could make them nice and smooth, and then I called the boys in for dinner.

You'll never guess what happened. One of those 3-year-old twins came traipsing in with the very bamboo spoon I remembered stirring the potatoes with, like I hadn't been using it first. He must have sent a ninja to do his dirty work, because when he's trying to steal books from the home library after lights out, his footfalls are so thunderous they resemble a herd of elephants fleeing whatever makes elephants run. I heard nothing this time around.

If it hadn't been so maddening, I would have been a little bit impressed.

I can't keep a house tidy, because boys keep swiping my stuff. They're like practiced thieves when it comes to things like wire whisks and flashlight batteries and the last of the flour in the freezer. The other day, I found a metal nut cracker upstairs in their room, because they "wanted to see what happened when you use it on a bouncy ball" (sadly, the ball is no longer with us). I will find perfectly good table spoons out in the backyard, because they "wanted to see how long it would take to dig to the earth's mantle using a silver spoon" (You never actually get there, because there's too much limestone in our soil. And it would take twelve hundred years.). I will find random things in the freezer, because someone wanted to know "what would happen to a glass mixing bowl when you fill it with water and put an old banana in the middle of it and freeze it."

Tell me, please, how it's remotely possible to keep a clean and tidy house when you don't even know where half your possessions are? The 8-year-old has broken into our bedroom while both of us were occupied by boys downstairs and stolen paperclips, because he wanted to clip all his papers together, and by the time we found him, he had a string of a hundred paperclips already wrapped around each other, because, in his words, when he looked at that paperclip in just the right way, he realized that he could string them all together and that would make a really cool decoration for his room, which he plans to put…

On the floor.

Boys use forks to try to dig out rocks, no matter how many times you tell them to keep what's inside inside (and no matter how many times you almost curse because you just stuck a prong up your nose while the rest went in your mouth, where they're supposed to go). They will use butter knives to carve boxes into houses and leave the knives on the table instead of putting them back away so the next time we need to spread butter or jam on something, there's no utensil left that will work. They will use baby spoons to pretend that their stuffed animals are eating something tasty, and when you need to feed the real live baby in your house, those three metal spoons have disappeared into the black hole of a 5-year-old's room.

And the most annoying part of it all is that you won't even know those things are missing until you finally need them, which for some things is a relatively long time. I didn't notice the foil was gone until I had a dish, months later, that didn't have a lid, and I needed to use it to cover our leftovers. And when I asked the boys if they had seen the 500-foot roll of foil anywhere, the 8-year-old brought it back downstairs and said he'd been using it to "make a person out of a toilet paper roll."

There are so many things that disappear in a house with children, and they will not turn up until you're kneeling down on the floor and that missing object comes out to maul you in some way. You will not realize your serving spoon went missing until you sit on the couch and you suddenly have bamboo up your bunghole. And then you'll wonder who in the world managed to lodge a spoon down the crack of the couch (and now in another crack) when they're not even allowed to eat in this room, and you'll never know, because they're too busy laughing at how it's perfectly wedged between your cheeks and you're, honestly, too busy trying to get it out and, after that, trying to walk back to the sink, because it may be easy to recover from an injury like that one when you're 8, but it's much harder when you're 30.

So, in a way, it's actually pretty hazardous to live with children, because they're always setting up traps for you. And I would be willing to bet they really like doing it, because it's pretty funny to see a mom limping around after stubbing her toe on a metal bowl that was hiding under a blanket she kicked in her frustration because it shouldn't have been on the floor, yet again. I guess it *is* pretty funny. I guess I can at least give them that.

But I cannot give them permission to use my household utensils for God knows what. I will have to draw my line there, because those are things I need. Seriously, kids. Stop trying to pretend your lunch containers are doggie bowls for your stuffed animals. If you want a lunch tomorrow at school, curb your creativity a little. I promise you'll find plenty of other supplies elsewhere, if you'll just get out of my kitchen.

What Happens When the Couch Cushions are Removed from the Couch

What's the point of couch cushions, you ask?

Well, that would be pulling them off the couches and spreading them all over the floor, of course.

In a home with children, the couch cushions are never where they're supposed to be, which is actually a good thing, in my opinion. Do you know how much stuff can get trapped under a couch? Trust me. They're doing you a huge favor.

When you crack down on couch cushions staying on the couch, you'll find all kinds of nastiness under the cushions. Like, for example, old M&Ms, and you don't even allow your kids to eat M&Ms, so there's no telling where THAT came from—probably the pocket of someone who came over to your house, except no one's been to your house in six months, which means that M&M your 3-year-old just ate is…ancient in candy age.

You'll also find old crayons caked with hair and gunk and all sorts of unidentified disgusting you didn't even know was there or how it got there in the first place. We don't allow eating on our couches, and somehow we still find petrified carrots in the cracks.

When my boys get a wild hair every other second and decide to strip the couches of their cushions so they can make a tent and sleep on the cushions tonight—we'll let them experience the effects of not sleeping tomorrow, since all we, their parents, want to do is go to bed ourselves—there is all kinds of nastiness unearthed.

It's weird, too, because they'll find coins, and I know for a fact that we don't carry coins, because we don't usually work with cash at all. The boys get a small allowance, so I guess it belonged to them in the first place.

We'll also find hair. Lots and lots of who-does-this-belong-to hair. It's probably mine, but some of it, caked with dust and whatever it is that gets smashed like gum between the cushions, has no apparent owner. If I allow myself time to think about this, I feel slightly unsettled, so I avoid using my imagination at all costs when it comes to the mysterious hair living under my couch cushions.

They will find old, broken crayons that have melted, possibly beneath the gas fumes of boys who sit on top of them during Family Movie Night. (What's that smell? You mean, besides noxious gas? That would be melting crayon.) They will find old library books for which we have already paid. They will find half-eaten carrots that someone must have snuck into the living room while we weren't looking. They will marvel at its wooden appearance.

They will find shoes that have been missing for ages, contorted in a way that doesn't resemble a shoe at all anymore. They will find old crumpled up papers no one even noticed were missing (because there are so many more, everywhere), including an old sheet from your premarital counseling days, when you made a lovely little circle with all the facets of marriage, including SEX, which they'll ask you about as soon as they're done reading the other words written on it. They will find old cough drop wrappings, because someone has a bad habit of never throwing things away and always asks his brother to do it, except he refuses to pay the brother for being his personal maid, so the wrapper gets crushed between the cushions. They will find crumbs of unidentifiable origins that now, in this advanced decomposition stage, look like nothing but dirt. They will find the permanent markers they used to write on these cushions and remember how it was so fun that they think they'll do it again when Mama and Daddy aren't looking.

All this to say that when boys take the cushions off couches, what they're really trying to do is help you, because, look, there's that old game piece that went missing. Too bad we already got rid of that game, and now there's just a random piece the 8-year-old wants to keep, because he wants to "remember that old game we used to play." And then when they score a penny or two, they will beg to go to the store, because they're rich—they have two coins!—and we will have to explain to them that pennies will hardly buy anything at all, at least not with today's inflation prices (Did a penny ever buy anything? I don't remember.).

And, yeah, it's maddening when you get ready to take a load off your feet and all the couches and chairs are emptied of their cushions and you don't even want to sit on that unidentified mess that's stuck underneath them, but then, if you're lucky and not too tired, you'll get a wild hair of your own and take a vacuum cleaner to those couches, and then it will be easy peasy to put those cushions back on and pretend you totally have it together, because *You just vacuumed your couches,* and who does that when they have kids? No one, that's who. Way to go, super mom.

So maybe we should look at this where-did-all-the-couch-cushions-go with new eyes and tell ourselves that our children are really, at the heart of them, trying to help us improve our own tidying and cleaning practices, because they've just emptied the couches of their cushions and pulled out its buried treasures, and all we have to do is get the vacuum cleaner out. They did all the heavy lifting. That's something to be thankful for, right?

Right. Now get to work.

Bath Toys: Also Known as 'The Harborer of a Good Mold Colony'

Who invented bath toys? I mean, they're great creations. My boys get to spray each other in the face with them so I can hear their voices every other second tattling on who did it this time. And they get to dump bucketfuls of water out of the bathtub because my reflexes are too slow when I figure out what's on their minds. And they get to fight over the same seal even though there are twelve other animals for the two of them in the bath. Like I said, bath toys are great creations.

We used to have these bath toys that spit water and made washing the soap off my boys wonderfully easy and fun. And they would always laugh about the pirate spitting on them, as if cleaning were a game, which I suppose is always the goal when you're a parent trying to wash cakes of dirt from your boys because they only take baths every other day, and everybody knows that kids who take a bath every other day are really dirty kids.

(Not really. People just like to believe that, because they like making parents think they're not doing their best. It's only sweat. Never killed anybody. If I really wanted to get my boys clean, I would have to wash them forty times a day, because it never fails that two seconds after their bath, they will find some dirt to rub all over their faces. Or snot. They're really good at the rubbing-snot-on-their-faces thing, and most of the time they're crying when they get out of the bath, even though they no longer have bath toys and it's not really all that fun anymore. But we're getting to that.)

Back when we only had three kids, we had a bathtub full of toys, and boys would play for several minutes, until our timer went off and we had to tell them it was time to get out and all of them would start screaming the same words they'd said last night, after they'd played for several minutes: "But I never get to play!" We took these little displays in stride, knowing that once we settled in for reading time, they would forget all about how much fun they had in the bath.

In the beginning, we were diligent. After each bath, when our boys were done with the bath toys for the night, we would meticulously clean them up and put the back in the little baskets on the side of the bath tub, making double sure to squeeze all the extra water out of them.

And then this effort, after all of three days, began to fizzle out, because what was the point of putting bath toys away, if the boys were just going to play with them again tomorrow (or the day after that)? We were fortunate not to have to share a shower with them, so it didn't really matter that there were toys all over the bottom of the tub, because we wouldn't, after all, have to step over a thousand squishy pirates to take our shower and they would be able to play with them without asking us to get them down. Still, we would squeeze all the water out of them, even though I knew in the back of my mind and just didn't let myself think too long about the fact that there was still water that perpetually clung to the sides of those toys and never dried out, which is the preferred conditions for growing mold. All those toys came with their claims that they were made with material that wouldn't mildew, but how is anything that spends its life waterlogged going to avoid mildew and mold?

If they were, in fact, made of material that repelled mildew, it didn't work with our kind of mildew. Or maybe it's because we gave up on the cleaning of them.

So they started smelling, of course.

It's kind of like that nose thing that you use to suck out all the snot that could possibly be held in an infant's sinus cavity. You start out really well cleaning it every time you use it, and then you realize how much you actually have to use it, because kids and snot could be synonymous, and you stop caring after a while. It's just going to get snot in it tomorrow. Why should you clean it out today?

After a while, your diligence slips. You realize your baby isn't going to die just because you didn't clean out the snot collector. You realize they're also not going to die because you didn't wash out the bath toys.

And then came the time when one of the boys filled up that open-mouthed pirate with a bellyful of water, and when he squeezed it, unknown and unidentifiable chunks shot out of the pirate's piehole, and I threw up in my mouth and grabbed all the toys from the boys and said we'd put them away for another day, and then, when they had all fallen asleep, I packed them up in a black trash bag and took them directly out to the curb so my boys would never know what had happened to them (Husband and I are like reverse Santa Clauses. We don't bring toys. We make toys disappear. It's quite the talent.).

The next time they had a bath, my boys wondered where the toys were, but I brought some Hot Wheels up, which don't have cavities that can't be explored, and they adjusted just fine. The 8-year-old, every now and then, still talks about those pirate toys that disappeared one day when he was 4, and even though he's too old to play with them now, he wishes he had them "for his baby brothers," because he's kind like that, and, also, he would pretend he was playing with his brothers when he was really playing himself.

So maybe eventually we'll invest in another set of bath toys. Probably not.

When the Outdoors Come Creeping In

We have a large backyard with a fence built around it, and it's contained and safe, which means my boys spend a whole lot of time in it, sometimes with the back door locked and sometimes not.

They will jump on the trampoline, and they will play on the swing set, and they will mostly dig holes.

This digging holes used to be a thing we didn't allow, because there are sprinklers in the backyard, but the sprinklers gave up years ago when Husband found a leak and started digging and ruptured a line that sprayed his face so hard his glasses flew fifty feet over the back of the fence. We had always intended on getting them fixed, but then we saw how many holes the boys had carved in our lawn, and we decided it would probably be more prudent to wait. Why would we want to water dirt in the backyard, anyway? That sounds like a recipe for a mama carted off to the loony bin, because mud. And boys. I don't need to say any more.

My point in all this, though, is to say that there is hardly one instance in the transition between outdoor play and indoor play when dinner needs to be eaten or baths need to be taken or stories need to be read that a part of the outside doesn't come in.

Sometimes this looks like a tree branch the boys thought looked really nice, so they ripped it from the tree and brought it in to put with their dress-up clothes, because they have a Robin Hood costume, and this branch looks like the start of a curved bow.

Sometimes this looks like the colorful things they pick in our yard that they call flowers but are really just weeds. Sometimes it looks like rocks they tote home from the schoolyard, because they love collecting rocks for no purpose whatsoever.

Mostly, though, it's dirt and bugs.

Not long ago I was cleaning out my pantry, and I was transferring some almonds into mason jars instead of keeping them in their plastic pouches, and I found what I thought was an empty mason jar. I took it to the sink, thinking I probably needed to wash it, because it hadn't been used in a while. Upon closer inspection, I realized that it was a graveyard for roly polies (otherwise known as pillbugs). Someone, apparently, had been collecting them one day and then forgot all about them.

Yesterday I was doing dishes, and I noticed that one of the cups had dirt in it, because not only does the outside tend to come in, but the inside tends to also, mysteriously, go out, so I ran some water in it, and then I realized that there was a tiny little LIVE snail floating in the water, and I felt so bad that someone had brought a tiny little snail inside and I had been the one to kill it.

And then there are the times they bring spiders in with them, because they're really just harmless Daddy Long Legs, which aren't even spiders at all, except I really hate anything that resembles spiders, and I'll screech around the house once they've dropped it in my lap, and they become forever terrified of spiders because of my unexpected response.

There are always grass remnants on the ground and mud on the floors and interesting leaves in the key tray by the front door, and there are always sticks they bring in because one of them makes a great staff and another makes a great whip and another of them just looked interesting. I find these things all over the floor and stuffed under the couches and in my bed.

Not too long ago I slipped under my covers and heard a crunch under my backside. It was a leaf the 6-year-old wanted to show me, because it was shaped like a heart. It broke like his heart, and he didn't think it was too funny when I pointed out that it looked a lot like his heart at that moment, because he'd lost a leaf that looked like a heart, and then I had to empathize and understand and, mostly, apologize for my careless getting into bed. You'd think by now I'd know to check before I lie down.

I find sticker burrs attached to socks when I'm trying to sort the laundry, and then it's not just sticker burrs attached to socks, because I didn't know those socks had sticker burrs in them before I put them in the wash with all the other dirty clothes, so now we have sweaters with sticker burrs and sweatpants with sticker burrs, and, most annoying and painful of all, my sports bras with sticker burrs. I don't usually notice this last one until the bra is on and I'm wondering why it feels like there are nails in my chest. Sticker burrs don't stay contained to socks when they're tumbling around in a washing machine and then a dryer, and the more dried out they get, the deeper they burrow into those clothes.

It doesn't matter how many times I tell them to leave the outside where it is happiest—outside—they will bring it all inside, either intentionally because they like to have that reminder of the Great Outdoors or unintentionally because they have no idea that their socks were covered in burrs.

On my good and patient days, I find this bringing-in-the-Great-

Outdoors kind of neat, because our house doesn't need all those typical seasonal decorations you can buy for half price at Hobby Lobby. It now has enough outdoor decorations of its own. So what if it's a dying branch and some dried-out leaves and a little graveyard of roly polies? It means that we can look at those things and remember the good times we had in the beautiful, wide-open space of Mother Nature.

But ask me what I think tomorrow, when I have to sweep the kitchen for the fortieth time in two hours.

The Only Word I Have for Play-Doh: Why?

Tonight my boys brought home some balls of Play-Doh from church.

Baby boy was sick, so I didn't have the privilege of going with them to their class, where they got to make some really cool things and play some really cool games and, in general, get all hyped up about being at church, the greatest place ever, which is kind of the point for us, but I did get to see one thing they made: Play-Doh sculptures. One of them made a scorpion, one of them made a robot, and the other made something unidentifiable (he doesn't even know). It doesn't really matter was it was. What matters is that as soon as they got home, they stuck it in my face, even though I've told them a million times that I don't like people putting things in my face, especially when it's Play-Doh, and I felt my stomach drop a little with that dread every parent knows.

Ugh. Play-Doh.

You see, I have this love-hate relationship with Play-Doh. On the one hand, it's really great for kids. They get to play with something they can mold and control and make out of it whatever their little hearts want to make. It's great for art, great for interaction, and great for fine motor skills. So many benefits. I know all these benefits, and I have friends who make their homemade Play-Doh and let their kids play with it all the time. But my kids, well, they rarely, if ever, get to play with Play-Doh.

One time someone thought Play-Doh would make the perfect birthday gift for one of my boys, and I promptly put that considerate and kind gift into a brown sack and packed it away in our pantry, because out of sight, out of mind, and maybe if they couldn't see it, they would forget they had ever gotten it, and I would never have to see Play-Doh (or hear about it) again.

I don't know if maybe my aversion goes back to when I was a kid and my brother dared me to eat some Play-Doh and I did, and it was the nastiest thing in the world (even though my kids would tell you differently) so I can't even smell it today without gagging. I don't think that's it, because I'm pretty tough, and I'm sure I could suck this up.

I think what it really comes down to is the crumbs.

The tiny little dried-out crumbs. The tiny little dried-out crumbs that get stuck all over your feet because you were too tired the night they were playing with the Play-Doh to make the grand effort of sweeping it all up, plus it was still wet, and the only thing worse than dried Play-Doh crumbs is wet Play-Doh crumbs sticking all over your broom so they fall off every time you try to sweep again.

When it's time to clean up Play-Doh, there is no clean-up of Play Doh. Kids will stuff different colors together, which irks you in the slightest, because maybe you're a little neurotic. And they will pick up all the crumbs they can see from the table, so the yellow is dotted with blue and green and hot pink, and then they will stuff a blob that's bigger than a container into a container, and they will try to smash the lid onto it, but it doesn't work, of course, because the blob is too big, and then you'll have to help them by cutting the blob in half, except there's nowhere else for it to go but in the container with the red. Now your neurotic self just started crying inside, but what else are you going to do? Besides, one of them will most likely grab it and stuff it in anyway, so here. You do it.

And they're pretty good at getting all the specks off the table, but they won't even check under the table, and all you know is that when they get down from the table and go up to their rooms, because they're finished cleaning, there's a string of purple specks smashing into the carpet, and you know you'll never be able to get that out until it thoroughly dries.

So then you think that tomorrow morning you'll sweep it all up, except you know what it's like in the mornings. There's so much to do already, because there are children to wake and remind over and over and over again to get out of their beds so they can then get dressed and brush their teeth and leave for school, because you sure need a break. You'll never have time to sweep.

And just thinking about all that's in store for you leaves you so exhausted you can't even pick up the broom, so there the little tiny pieces stay, probably to be later found by your infant, who's just started moving. He'll clean them up faster than any Hoover could.

This is why my kids don't play with Play Doh. So when they brought their creations home from church and proudly showed them off to me, I took them and stuffed them in that brown sack, because out of sight, out of mind has worked before and maybe it will again.

Besides, what does anyone need with dried Play Doh creations, anyway?

The Amazing Things that End Up in the Laundry

I used to hear stories from parents about the funny things that ended up in their kids' laundry, and I always thought I'd never be one of those. I'd check all the pockets and make sure my boys never hid anything in them.

And then I became a parent, and I realized, as we so often do, that my expectations were a little too high, because parenting was a whole lot harder than I thought, and so was doing laundry for eight people. Already it takes me half an hour just to sort laundry, because not only do my boys forget to put laundry in the hamper, but they also forget to turn it right side out. (We'll work on getting it to the hamper first. I feel like that's all I can expect for now.) Ain't nobody got time to check pockets, too.

It's not just the pockets, either. I sort laundry downstairs, and it's amazing what those piles attract before they actually get put in the wash.

For your entertainment purposes, I thought I would list the most frequent findings in my laundry:

Shoes. I'm not really sure how this happens. The best I can understand is that there are piles in the living room, and someone comes in from outside and kicks off his shoes like a little football player punting a ball, except this is a shoe. That's still on his foot. The shoes, of course, go every which way, and some of them get in a pile of clothes. And then the pile of clothes is pushed around a little, because boys aren't very mindful of what they're stepping on while they're walking (they don't even notice the LEGOs sometimes, which is quite a feat, in my opinion), and before you know it, two shoes are sitting in the pile of dark clothes. And when I pick up the laundry and put it in the basket to cart it over to the washer, maybe it does feel a little heavier than normal, but, honestly, the only thing I want to do is get started and finished in this year, so I don't even pay attention. Typically those shoes are wrapped pretty efficiently into a long-sleeved shirt or a pair of jeans, almost like the clothes don't really want to let it go and so I wouldn't notice it, anyway, even if I were looking. Crazy shoes. This is probably why we have so many left feet in our house—because the washed shoes go the same route as the missing socks.

I'll typically discover the presence of a shoe in the laundry by the massive thumping it's doing as it spins round and round, like it's panicked about all that energy efficient heat so it starts knocking on the sides of the dryer to escape. The thought process often goes like this:

Me, to myself: What's that noise?

[Look around. The boys are at the table, coloring. No one is thumping.]

[Peer outside the back door, because there's probably some kind of vermin trying to get inside.]

Me, to myself: We did smell a skunk last night. I bet it's probably a crazed skunk, in which case I need to know about him so I don't let the boys out to play. Don't want any rabies passed around the house.

Me, to myself: Oh, man, what if it *is* a crazed skunk and half the boys are missing in action? What if they're out jumping on the trampoline? Did I hear them go out the back door?

Me, to myself: Wait. It's coming from the pantry. Is there something in the garage? Geez. I don't even want to know. Remember when we had an invasion of field mice? Bleh. Someone else is going to have to find out.

I'll just peek for a minute.

Wow. It's so loud.

And rhythmic.

Oh. It's the dryer. A shoe.

Roly Polies. They were alive once. One of my 3-year-olds enjoys collecting roly polies. Usually he'll just bring them in the house and put them in a small pile that no one else knows about, so (hopefully) the roly polies escape back out into the yard. Sometimes he puts them in jars and makes a little bug graveyard, because they don't last long and he forgets about them. Sometimes he puts them in his pocket. This is how they end up in the laundry. There aren't many of them, as far as I can see. But they're stuck tight. And if I know the boy who picked them up and put them in his pocket, there were a hundred of them to begin with, and the rest of them are either in the lint filter or somewhere down the drain of the washer. Poor bugs.

Crayons. This is a pretty common one for parents. I'm not telling you anything new. Thankfully, we wash our clothes on the cold cycle, and so the crayons don't melt and get all over the clothes. Someone would be in a lot of trouble if they did.

Pens, pencils and other drawing supplies. Typically we'll avoid the drawing-all-over-clothes, because we don't use heat in the washer, and, also, they're easy enough to notice before the transfer to the dryer. This is because our washer shakes them silly before it stops.

Coins. I've got a whole essay on coins and how I have no idea how they get into my house, because we don't use cash for anything. Go read that. It's like I'm running a laundromat in the opposite direction. Put the clothes in, get the coins out. Too bad pennies take a long time to make you rich.

Tiny scraps of paper. I guess the boys like crumbling up paper and stuffing it in their pockets, because I find these just about every single laundry day. I don't know if they're love notes or just notes in general, but the thought of love notes makes me think maybe I should start checking all the pockets after all. The only recipient of a love note should be me.

Stuffed animals. Sometimes this is because the boys decided they wanted to wash their stuffies, because Pinkabul really needs a bath, and sometimes it's unintentional, because they have so many stuffed animals they don't even know what to do with them all. Regardless, I hardly ever know about it, except by the cracking I hear coming from the laundry room, because they only collect Beanie Boos with the gigantic, creepy eyes. It's like a heart-attack waiting to happen when I hear those cracks, because I know I'll open the washer and pull out a near-drowned fox looking at me with eyes that are bigger than mine. Those are my favorite.

Hats, mittens and scarves. In the middle of a Texas summer. Generally, this is because they don't put these things back where they go when they took them out to play dress-up in the air-conditioned house. They'll see the piles of clothes all sorted and think it would be easier to put them in the laundry than back where they go. I know, because this is the same exact thing they do with clothes that fall off their hangers in their rooms. It doesn't matter if they haven't been worn in months, those pants will end up in the laundry. Husband does this, too, so I guess they get it honest.

Stickers. This one's delightful, because when you realize you've missed a sticker on a shirt, and you go to pull it off, it leaves all the residue for you. And you'll make sores on your fingers trying to get all the residue off. So, like I said, please stop giving us stickers.

I know I need to be better about checking the boys laundry before I throw it in the wash, but with eight loads of laundry to do every week, let me ask you, would you?

What Stickers Can Teach Us About Persistence

My gosh. I am so tired of stickers I want to put a sign on our door that says, "If you come bearing stickers, do not cross this threshold."

People who buy my kids coloring books with stickers in them, because this is so much cooler than a regular coloring book? Please stop. People who think my kids will surely love this package of three thousand stickers (of course they will. Who doesn't like annoying their mom with a sticker on every inch of her bedroom wall?)? Please stop. People who think maybe we could use these leftover motivational stickers for chore charts or potty training? Stop.

There was a time, not so long ago, when we thought that stickers would be a fun idea. I remember loving stickers as a kid. What I don't remember is sticking them everywhere, but something I've learned about my boys is that even if we provide them with a sheet of paper to put their stickers on, that's not where they will end up. Instead, they will end up on shirts and couches and floors and tables and usually my monstrous behind without my knowledge.

The first time we bought stickers, our first son was 2. We were potty training him, and we wanted to have a progress chart, because he was a bright boy and could figure out the calendar thing, counting how many days he'd stayed dry and clean. He was potty trained within a couple of weeks. So when it came time to potty train boy #2, we thought stickers would be a good idea again. Except we forgot that there was an older boy in the house who still loved stickers and wouldn't be getting any, because he was not the one potty training.

We found stickers everywhere. I mean, everywhere.

And even though now we have vowed to ban stickers from our house, we still find them everywhere.

The other day we went to the store to get some more coloring books, because our 3-year-olds love coloring, and I love keeping their hands busy, because, otherwise, they're reaching for knives when I'm not looking or deconstructing the bread machine when I take a potty break or trying to carry their baby brother by his neck when I turn around to make lunch. Most of the coloring books with uncolored pages in our house belong to their older brothers, because the twins have pretty much scribbled on every one of the pages of their own books and called it done.

I looked at so many coloring books. I was hard-pressed to find one that didn't promise "Fifty brand new stickers."

What in the world? Are coloring books not enough anymore? We have to entice kids to sit down and color with the promise of stickers? I DON'T WANT STICKERS IN MY HOUSE.

Stickers, you see, get EVERYWHERE.

Have you ever gone all the way to your boys' school to pick them up after the bell rings and been told, politely, that you have an "awesome job" sticker on your rump, as if someone just wanted to tell you that you did a perfect job on those fifty squats earlier and smacked that sticker on you? I have. Have you ever walked into a grocery store with a Spider-Man sticker attached to the back of your head, because someone, while you weren't looking, decorated the headrest in the van, and you didn't realize it until you finally, just before leaving to go back home, looked behind you to see who was pulling your hair? Dang Spider-Man. Have you ever gone to a parent-teacher conference with Diego and his backpack staring at the teacher when you turned around because one of your kids thought it would be funny to stick it on your upper back, where you can't even reach it, when you weren't paying attention? I have.

And if I cared about what people thought, it would be terribly embarrassing. Since I don't care, it's just annoying.

So is opening the door to guests and turning back around to find a trail of Hulk stickers leading the way to the kitchen. So is hosting a birthday party and being asked if I'm aware that Iron Man is staring at everyone in the bathroom, because he's stuck on every available surface of the walls. So is pulling up to the pediatrician's office and opening the van door to take out my 3-year-old and seeing that he's got puppies plastered all over his face.

Stickers are not my friend. We didn't learn from the first disaster and stubbornly used stickers to potty train all our boys (because the hope that "this one will be different" is hard to kill), and, inevitably, someone would raid those reward stickers and slap A+ and Superb! all over the floor and we'd have to spend hours peeling them off. It didn't matter how high we'd put that little book of stickers, little boys would scale walls to get them. I don't even know how they did it, because I had to stand on tiptoe to reach them, but somehow they did, and every single time those stickers ended up in places they shouldn't have been. On library books. All over the toilet seat. Up on the ceiling.

One time I went into my twins' room to get them up from their nap and found stickers on their blinds, their closet door, their mirror, their lamp, their dresser, their chair, their bed frame, their door frame, and every available inch of skin. Everywhere. It's still a mystery how they smuggled the booklet of stickers in with them. I peeled them all off, cursing in my head, but of course the stickers left souvenirs—the white sticky part you have to scrub with alcohol to get off. Who has time for that? I don't even have time for showering anymore.

Needless to say, there are still some stickers on things. We haven't scraped them all off, because there are too many of them. And I'd like to save my efforts for the prevention side of things: Keeping stickers out of the house in the first place.

So. No more stickers allowed. For real this time. Unless you want to be the one to come peel them off everything.

In that case, be my guest.

How Kids Manage to Lose Their Left Shoes

There is quite a mysterious phenomenon that happens when you have children: If something has a mate (like shoes), it will travel the farthest reaches of the earth (or home) to separate itself from its mate.

The only thing present in my mind at these moments of astonishing discovery is: How?

You'll often ask yourself this "how" question when your kids walk right out of their shoes, and the next day the shoe's mate can't be located. It's five minutes to leaving time before you'll have to write another tardy note to the front office, and they're still looking for a lost shoe. They found one of them by the front door and have been looking for its mate for twenty minutes, which is also how long you've been listening to him whine about not being able to find his shoes. The mate is finally, finally located behind the chair that sits on the other side of the room.

You'll ask yourself this question when you're telling your 3-year-old to get his shoes and socks on, and he's saying he doesn't have socks, except you specifically remember getting him brand new socks recently. And then you'll find one sock stuffed in a shoe (and it's wet!) and the other sock sloped across their brother's backpack by the front door, even though you remember putting both of them in the living room, right by his clothes set out for the day.

And if they happen to play sports, you'll have the privilege of finding one shin guard, and the other will go missing somewhere else, because it is impossible for kids to put things where they go. It doesn't matter if you have a designated place for those shin guards, they will never get there.

You'll often wonder how a pair of anything could get so widely separated, and then you'll watch your kid walk through the door and kick off one shoe, which lands right beside the front door, and kick off the other, which will land, like a football he's just punted, all the way across the room, missing the fan by half an inch (and that's a lucky day). You'll watch your kid sit down with his socks and then forget entirely what he's doing and carry the sock over to the shoes and put it down while he searches for the right shoe, because, surprise, surprise, it's not anywhere near the left shoe, and then he will move back to where he left the sock he hasn't yet touched, and he'll see there's only one here because, remember, he left the other one by the front door, except he doesn't know he left the other one by the front door, so he's just going to holler about how you only gave him one sock, and don't you know he needs two socks? And you'll quietly walk to the sock beside the door and pick it up and hand it to him, and he won't even know—*he won't even know*—that he's the very one who put it there. He'll blame you.

You will watch another kid run into the house and stumble over the one shoe he's taken off. He's still wearing the other, and he's headed straight to the bathroom, so you know very well not to say a thing, because it's more important that he reaches the bathroom before it's too late, and when he comes out there are no more shoes, so you know there's one by the door and one in the bathroom, but he'll forget in another three seconds.

"Did you make it?" you'll say.

He'll look at you like you're crazy, because of course he did, and then he's on his way back outside. He just needs his shoes. There's one by the front door, but where is the other?

"Where are my shoes?" he'll say. "I put them right here."

I beg to differ.

How does it happen? It happens with living. Kids aren't so good about stopping and taking things off all at the same time or putting those taken off things in their proper place. Even if they've had a thousand mornings of shoe searching and our answer, on repeat, is always, "Well, we have a shoe basket where the shoes go. You should work harder to get your shoes into the basket, and then you won't have to search so hard for them all the time," chances are they'll completely forget tomorrow, as soon as they walk through the door and remember how much they missed their Hot Wheels and all they really want to do, right this minute, is sit down and play with them, or they really need to use the bathroom or they are too excited about jumping on the trampoline to be bothered with remembering where their shoes and socks belong.

There's plenty of time for them to learn to slow down enough to do it right, to put things in their proper place. They won't be losing their shoes forever.

Or maybe I'm just kidding myself.

One Day They Will Be Gone

One day the grass will grow green and perfect and true

One day you will not step in a humongous hole in the backyard wilderness and nearly break your foot

One day the nicks in the walls will be smoothed, and the accidental holes will be patched and the paint will be reapplied without a finger touching it too soon

One day the couches will not fall apart when you sit on them

One day the chairs will all be pushed in

One day the dishes will get put away and loaded into a dishwasher every single day

One day their rooms will not have a carpet of clothes on the floor

One day the entryway will not be strewn with shoes

One day the living room will not look like a toy factory exploded

One day their books won't lie all over the floor, waiting to be re-shelved

One day there won't be a pile of food on the floor beneath our table that looks like it could feed an entire country

One day their artwork won't be left on our pillow because they wanted to make sure we saw it before we went to bed

One day there won't be a massive stack of papers to be sorted every day

One day there won't be toothpaste smeared all over the counters

One day there won't be letters practiced on bathroom mirrors
One day there won't be surprises in the laundry
One day the spills won't cake counters and cabinets
One day we won't find stickers on every available surface of their bed
One day there won't be dress-up clothes scattered all over the living room
One day there won't be one shoe where it's supposed to be and one clear out the back door
One day we won't wonder where the wooden spoon went
One day we will be able to walk on any floor surface of our house without LEGOs puncturing our feet or food sticking to the bottom of them
One day we will walk into our house and it will smell like cinnamon instead of swamp
One day all the new murals on our home walls will stop appearing
One day the couch pillows will stay put
One day the bathrooms in our house won't need the sign "Enter at your own risk"
One day we will be able to climb into bed without cutting our leg on a piece of bark they put there because they intended to show it to us, and then they forgot
One day we will be able to take a bath without a thousand toys needing to be put away
One day we will never have to look at Play Doh again
One day we will get rid of a toy and it will stay gone
One day we will be able to unpack our purse or backpack every

time we walk through the door, if we so desire

One day we will not have have to clean up tiny little pieces of paper they decided to cut up when they found the scissors

One day we will not have to navigate paper airplanes

One day we won't have spare change clanging all over the house

One day we won't look under their beds and find the missing lunch container that disappeared three months ago

One day we won't have an astounding stockpile of child artwork

One day we will have a tidy house

One day we will miss our untidy house and the bathrooms that smelled like they should have been Port a Potties and all the inconvenient marks of their presence

Because one day they'll be gone.

The End

Don't miss out on a Crash Test Parents release! Visit www.crashtestparents.com to keep up-to-date on book and product releases and to access bonus material.

Appendix A: The Folding Sock Technique that will Blow Your Mind

I had the book open, *The Life-Changing Magic of Tidying Up*, and I had reached the part where the author was explaining how to fold a sock, and I was thinking it was probably really stupid to fold a sock, but I wanted to try it anyway. But I guess I was trying too hard, making it all more complicated than it really was, because the directions provided in the book were somehow lost in translation.

I tried to fold, then I turned the socks over and tried to fold them again, and then I turned them over one more time and tried to fold. Finally, I just threw them across the room, because folding socks is stupid anyway.

It's just that this book had spoken to me. Have everything put away in its proper place. Yes. Of course that was the secret to a fulfilling life. Reduce your possessions to open your mind and a greater depth of creativity. Yes, of course I needed that.

Fold your socks.

I've never been a sock folder. All my life, I've put two socks together and let one of them swallow the other, so they're more a bulge than a fold. This, as you can imagine (and as the author so eloquently pointed out) results in stretched out ankles (or knees when I was in the knee-high wearing stage). And then I became a parent, and the dryer kept eating perfectly good socks, and there were never any matches to my kids' socks, so I made it easy on myself. I threw all the socks in a single drawer and let my boys fend for themselves in a giant battle of matching.

So I read this passage on folding socks with great interest, because I'd never known there was an *art* to it. This was what I had missed all my life.

There were a lot of things I used to do before I had kids. I used to iron shirts. I used to wash Husband's collared shirts and immediately set up the ironing board so I could get rid of all the wrinkles (this was before he told me that I ironed his shirts the wrong way, at which point I told him that he could just iron his own shirts from here on out. We'd been married a month. He never told me I did anything wrong again, but he still irons his own clothes.). And then we had kids, and most of our clothes ended up on the floor anyway, because, at the close of a day, we were too tired to put anything away, which means we walk around most days looking like we're wearing reused tissue paper.

I used to actually fold the boys' pajamas and shorts and jeans so all they had to do was put them away, but now it would take me as long as it takes Husband to do his hair in the morning to fold all the pieces in eight loads of laundry every week. So I put it in piles and let my kids put it away however they want (usually that means it's stuffed hilariously tight in their drawers, and then they complain that they can't open their drawers anymore or they can't find anything.).

I used to mend buttons when they went missing, and now I just teach my kids how to wear shirts without buttons, because it's the cool thing to do, and, also, mending buttons is way too time-consuming for a working mom of six.

There are so many of them and so few of me.

But, I don't know, there is something appealing and weirdly satisfying about folding your socks. To have them waiting, all lined up just so in a drawer. I would be able to see them all and not just the ones on top. I wanted this badly. I needed to know how. I tried again. Didn't work.

I put it aside and went back to my writing, because I had no more time for decoding someone else's ridiculously complicated instructions that didn't make the least bit of sense. I'd show Husband later, even though he probably wouldn't be able to figure it out either, since I'm definitely the smarter one in this partnership.

So, later, after we'd put the boys to bed and everyone was tucked away in their rooms, I finished sorting my clothes and mentioned to Husband my frustrating encounter with the art of folding socks.

It was written poorly, I said. I had read it several times and still couldn't understand what she was trying to say. Probably because the first printing wasn't done in English. Someone thought they were being clear in the translation, but they really weren't.

"Let me see the book," Husband said, like he couldn't believe that someone would possibly print something that didn't make the least bit of sense. I'm an author. I know it happens all the time.

I handed it over, though, knowing that if *I* couldn't figure it out, *he* most definitely wouldn't be able to figure it out. He smiled at me. I smiled back. Yeah, right, babe, I thought. You're going to be just as frustrated as I am.

So it was with a self-satisfied smirk that I walked over to the bookshelf and started rifling through another book I was reading. He was quiet for a few seconds. Probably going over and over in his mind what the author could possibly mean, like I had.

"Let me see your socks," Husband said after about a minute.

I put the other book back on the shelf, walked over to my side of the bed and threw two socks at him. "Let's see you work your magic," I said, confident that this was going to end the same way it had for me.

"This is going to blow your mind," he said. He put the two socks together, one on top of the other, folded them in half, and then handed them back to me.

"No," I said. "That's not how you do it."

He grinned at me, trying his best not to laugh.

"That's not all you have to do," I said. "There's no way that's all she was saying. You must not have read the same passage I read."

He handed me the book. I read the passage again. I looked at my socks, back at the book, back at the socks, and, finally, at Husband's face.

See, the thing I didn't want to admit is that he was right. He'd done exactly what she told her readers to do. Put the socks together. Fold them in half.

I was making it way more complicated than it really was. That's just because I have a much more advanced brain.

At least that's what I told myself as I turned away to put the perfectly folded socks into my dresser drawer.

Appendix B: The Criteria Necessary to Throw Out Your Kids' Books

When I was cleaning out our home's books, I started with what I thought would be the easy ones: the children's books. The problem is, though, that I'm a children's book author, so these are the books I love the most, naturally. I kept coming across books with broken bindings and would think, "We can fix this. I'm going to keep it." And then, "I don't really care for this story, but what if one of the boys does? I can't throw it away if there's a possibility they will want to read it and fall in love with it." And then, "Maybe this one just needs another chance. We'll read it again and see."

I'd sort more, and I would pause and think, hey, this is the book we read to the twins when they were in the NICU, and it talks about how each toe and finger and nose is unique but they were identical, so their daddy and I laughed hysterically at the irony of it. And this is the book we read to the oldest all the time when he was younger, over and over and over again, including that time we took it with us on a trip to Florida and he threw up all over it while we were taxiing down the airplane runway and all those people could smell the vomit, but not as much as we could, because it was all over us. And this is the book the second son picked out that day at Half Price Books for finishing his summer reading list, and even though it's a terrible story, he would be devastated if we got rid of it. Plus, it's 3D. Every boy's dream.

So the to-keep pile ended up way, way, larger than the get-rid-of-pile. In fact, there were only three books I was going to throw out, and it was because you couldn't turn a page without it falling out. I put all the books back on the shelf, thinking I'd try again later when I wasn't in such a nostalgic mood.

I thought it would be easier to toss out some of the picture books, but, boy was I wrong.

I don't want to give away the favorites, and I don't even know if I'll be able to part with them when my kids are grown. Mostly because I absolutely love picture books. I love the rhyming ones and the silly ones and the board ones with really neat pictures. I knew that I had to come at this project with a little bit of criteria, so I ticked off a few get-rid-of-them things in my mind.

1. The story isn't all that great.

If reading a book over and over again is worse than being the only adult in a room with five 3-year-olds for a whole afternoon, it needs to be tossed. And, sadly, a few of them met that criterion.

This was not a parents-don't-like-it-so-get-rid-of-it exercise. One of my least favorite stories is *Skippyjon Jones*, not because the story isn't brilliant but because I don't like all the voices I have to do (maybe once a year. But every day?). The kids expect those voices, because Husband has trained them to. He has a much better Spanish accent than I do, so this is typically what reading *Skippyjon Jones* looks like when I'm on duty:

Me: My name is Skippito Bandito—

Them: That's not how Daddy reads it.

Me: I don't care how Daddy reads it. This is how I read it.

Them: But you have to have more of an accent.

Me: Show me.

Them: [reading in the exact same voice as their regular voice] See?

Me: No.

Them: [rolling their eyes] We'll just ask Daddy to read it later.

Me: That's right. You will.

Don't get me wrong. *Skippyjon Jones* is a great story, but it's just not for me.

Where was I? Oh, yeah, this isn't just a parents-don't-like-it-so-get-rid-of-it exercise. There are still plenty of stories on our shelves that I don't really like reading, because they're either too long or they have too many other voices or I just don't like them for some unexplainable reason. Sorry, *Hotrod Hamster*. You did not make the cut.

2. The book binding is broken.

It was hard to add this to the criteria. Most of the broken binding books were ones our boys have loved well, but I knew we couldn't just keep them around indefinitely when they were missing pages or covers. Otherwise, the whole house would be overtaken by books, eventually. Plus, if they really miss them (and I do miss a lot of them), I'd get another copy.

Some of the favorites I kept in a basket in my closet, for future art projects, because I'm optimistic like that (and ridiculously unrealistic sometimes).

Those are the only rules I could make. And even after going through every single book in our home library with this criteria in mind, we were still left with thousands of picture books on the shelves.

Rachel Toalson

I guess this is what happens when you try to encourage people to get your kids books instead of toys for their birthdays. You end up with way more books than you'll ever need.

But we've read every one. So at least there's that.

Also, can there be too many books? I don't think so.

About the Author

Rachel is the COM (Chief Operating Maid) of the Toalson home, where she specializes in tossing nasty wet socks in their appropriate laundry pile, sorting through massive mounds of paper that collect on her kitchen counter, and trying to free her hand from the glue spot she didn't know was on her dining room table without ripping half her skin off (superglue is, of course, forbidden for use by unsupervised children, but her boys are persistent and crafty).

While she has loosened up considerably as a COM since becoming a mother, some things never die: Rachel still fights the daily battle against a paper-walled home, a floor made of clothes, and a bathroom that would make your nose hairs curl.

Rachel lives with her husband and six boys in San Antonio, Texas, where she faithfully writes at least 5,000 words a day, five days a week.

Author's Note

My dear reader,

I hope that in some small and maybe unexplainable way the words of this book have inspired or encouraged you. I believe there are more important things to do with the limited time we have with our children than worry so much about appearances. I hope that you have laughed right along with me about the impossibility and absurdity of attempting to keep a perfectly tidy house and that, rather than feeling like a failure for your tidying malfunction, you feel like you have permission to loosen up a little and maybe even enjoy (that might be a stretch, I know) all the ways your children thwart your efforts. They won't always be here, tearing up the world.

Husband and I sometimes look at each other when yet another thing in our house has fallen apart because of inappropriate use. "That's why we can't have nice things," we'll say, at almost exactly the same time (We've been married thirteen years. It's hard not to share a brain after all that time.). We'll follow that with "One day we'll be able to have nice things." But that "one day" only comes when our children are gone, and I want it to stay far away for as long as it possibly can.

I hope that you will move about your life mostly thankful for the nicks in your furniture and the drawings on walls you haven't yet had a chance to scrub off and the shoes separated by a powerful ninja kick, because one day you won't have to navigate the minefields of mess—and it will be deeply, achingly missed. Life with children flashes by. We may as well make the most of it.

If you can think of anyone who needs this book, please pass it along. Word of mouth is one of the most valuable ways a writer can share about her work.

Another valuable way to get this book into the hands of other readers is to write a review. It only takes a minute and a sentence (or two, if you're an overachiever like me).

Thank you for your support, and I'll see you back out in the trenches.

In love,
Rachel

Acknowledgements

While writing a book is a very solitary effort, a book is not begun and finished in solitude. Many heartfelt thanks go to:

My children, who provided all the real-life material within these pages. Even when it seems farfetched or fantastical, it is true. And I love you all madly for your wild and improbable ideas, experiments, and existences.

My husband, who agreed that this book needed to be written and who has always been my biggest and most faithful supporter.

All the friends who came over for dinner at our house, requiring us to perfect our Company Clean-up Checklist.

The random door ringers, who helped me feel more comfortable opening my door even if the house looked like someone had burglarized it.

The toys that keep coming back—you're funny. But get out.

The grandparents, who continue to bring our children more things.

My boys' school, which has yet to realize that we only need one copy of the registration for the Daddy Daughter dance—or, better yet, zero. (There are no daughters here.)

I love you all. Thank you for making this book possible.

Crash Test Parents

Enjoy more from the Crash Test Parents series:

www.crashtestparents.com

Are you a parent who needs a little dose of humor and hope?

For a limited time, pick up your FREE copies of *Guide to Surviving a Year* and *Guide to Self Esteem* and laugh your way back into hope. Or maybe just survival.

Get your FREE copies at:
racheltoalson.com/SurvivingAYear

www.ingramcontent.com/pod-product-compliance
Lightning Source LLC
Chambersburg PA
CBHW021431080526
44588CB00009B/491